The Hibernian magazine, or Compendium of entertaining knowledge, for ...

ECCO
PRINT EDITIONS

The Hibernian magazine, or Compendium of entertaining knowledge, for ...

Multiple Contributors, See Notes
ESTCID: P002405
Reproduction from Bodleian Library (Oxford)
Begun and published by James Potts, later published by Thomas Walker. Title and date repeated as caption at head of first page of text. Imprints lack dates; years of publication from dates of issues. Imprints vary; from <Nov.> 1772-Feb. 1773, imprint reads in part: printed by R[obert]. Marchbank for Peter Seguin; during 1773 imprint names alternate between Peter Seguin and James Potts, with printer John Lord's name also appearing in Apr. and May; from Nov. 1773-Feb. 1774 imprint reads: Printed by James Potts; from Mar. 1774 imprint reads in part: Printed by Thomas Walker, who by this time had taken over the publication. Title page includes list of contents. Printed in two columns. Text begins with factotum initial; ornamental headpiece above caption title of each issue. Running title includes subjects on current pages and date of issue. Issues include general essays on many topics, selections from literature, comments on the theatre, poetry, a summary of events in Europe and England for the month, public events in Ireland including marriage and death notices and promotions. During the American Revolution there is considerable coverage of events. Description based on: May, 1772.
Dublin [Ireland] : printed by James Potts, at Swift's-Head, in Dame-street.
v., plates (some fold.) : ill., tables, diagrs., maps, ports., music ; 8°

Gale ECCO Print Editions

Relive history with *Eighteenth Century Collections Online*, now available in print for the independent historian and collector. This series includes the most significant English-language and foreign-language works printed in Great Britain during the eighteenth century, and is organized in seven different subject areas including literature and language; medicine, science, and technology; and religion and philosophy. The collection also includes thousands of important works from the Americas.

The eighteenth century has been called "The Age of Enlightenment." It was a period of rapid advance in print culture and publishing, in world exploration, and in the rapid growth of science and technology – all of which had a profound impact on the political and cultural landscape. At the end of the century the American Revolution, French Revolution and Industrial Revolution, perhaps three of the most significant events in modern history, set in motion developments that eventually dominated world political, economic, and social life.

In a groundbreaking effort, Gale initiated a revolution of its own: digitization of epic proportions to preserve these invaluable works in the largest online archive of its kind. Contributions from major world libraries constitute over 175,000 original printed works. Scanned images of the actual pages, rather than transcriptions, recreate the works ***as they first appeared.***

Now for the first time, these high-quality digital scans of original works are available via print-on-demand, making them readily accessible to libraries, students, independent scholars, and readers of all ages.

For our initial release we have created seven robust collections to form one the world's most comprehensive catalogs of 18th century works.

Initial Gale ECCO Print Editions collections include:

History and Geography
Rich in titles on English life and social history, this collection spans the world as it was known to eighteenth-century historians and explorers. Titles include a wealth of travel accounts and diaries, histories of nations from throughout the world, and maps and charts of a world that was still being discovered. Students of the War of American Independence will find fascinating accounts from the British side of conflict.

Social Science

Delve into what it was like to live during the eighteenth century by reading the first-hand accounts of everyday people, including city dwellers and farmers, businessmen and bankers, artisans and merchants, artists and their patrons, politicians and their constituents. Original texts make the American, French, and Industrial revolutions vividly contemporary.

Medicine, Science and Technology

Medical theory and practice of the 1700s developed rapidly, as is evidenced by the extensive collection, which includes descriptions of diseases, their conditions, and treatments. Books on science and technology, agriculture, military technology, natural philosophy, even cookbooks, are all contained here.

Literature and Language

Western literary study flows out of eighteenth-century works by Alexander Pope, Daniel Defoe, Henry Fielding, Frances Burney, Denis Diderot, Johann Gottfried Herder, Johann Wolfgang von Goethe, and others. Experience the birth of the modern novel, or compare the development of language using dictionaries and grammar discourses.

Religion and Philosophy

The Age of Enlightenment profoundly enriched religious and philosophical understanding and continues to influence present-day thinking. Works collected here include masterpieces by David Hume, Immanuel Kant, and Jean-Jacques Rousseau, as well as religious sermons and moral debates on the issues of the day, such as the slave trade. The Age of Reason saw conflict between Protestantism and Catholicism transformed into one between faith and logic -- a debate that continues in the twenty-first century.

Law and Reference

This collection reveals the history of English common law and Empire law in a vastly changing world of British expansion. Dominating the legal field is the *Commentaries of the Law of England* by Sir William Blackstone, which first appeared in 1765. Reference works such as almanacs and catalogues continue to educate us by revealing the day-to-day workings of society.

Fine Arts

The eighteenth-century fascination with Greek and Roman antiquity followed the systematic excavation of the ruins at Pompeii and Herculaneum in southern Italy; and after 1750 a neoclassical style dominated all artistic fields. The titles here trace developments in mostly English-language works on painting, sculpture, architecture, music, theater, and other disciplines. Instructional works on musical instruments, catalogs of art objects, comic operas, and more are also included.

biblio life
old books. new life.

The great Sea Serpent

THE

HIBERNIAN MAGAZINE,

OR

Compendium of Entertaining Knowledge,

For FEBRUARY, 1771

TO THE PUBLIC

IT has been thought neceſſary by the Editors of the numerous Magazines with which of late years London teems, to addreſs the public with a circumſtantial and pompous detail of their propoſed plan all arrogating to themſelves ſome peculiar excellence, and each promiſing more entertainment than their predeceſſors, how far they have anſwered the expectations they raiſed, and how ſedulouſly they have adhered to their deſign is not for us to determine, their ſucceſs we think the beſt rule by which they may be judged

As for us, we ſhall not trouble you with a tireſome account of what we intend to write or to compile, let the matter ſpeak for itſelf, if it pleaſes, it is all we want, or you deſire, one thing only we ſhall intreat our brethren for, that is, to requeſt the correſpondence and aſſiſtance of the learned and witty of all denominations, whoſe favours we ſhall gratefully receive, with this caution only, that party or perſonal invective ſhall never find place with us

Some years ago an ingenious gentleman of the trade in this city, publiſhed a Magazine, which, not from want of merit or ſucceſs, but from ſome unaccountable fatality, he thought proper to drop, juſt when he had the faireſt proſpect of eſtabliſhing it, how could it be otherwiſe, being the firſt and only periodical production on an enlarged plan that had as yet been attempted in this city? and are we to ſuppoſe the capital of this kingdom, the ſecond in the Britiſh Empire, could not find ſale for one magazine? the contrary is obvious, as great numbers are monthly imported, the matter of many little deſerving your favour

Theſe reaſons have encouraged us to this undertaking, if we meet with your approbation, we ſhall, with unremitting care, continue our labours, if not, we ſhall at leaſt have this conſolation, that we meant well

Curious Account of that ſtrange Monſter, the great Sea Snake, as related by PONTOPPIDAN, *Biſhop of* BERGEN, *in his Natural Hiſtory of* NORWAY

THE See Ormen, the ſea ſnake, *Serpens Marinus Magnus*, called by ſome in this country the Aale-Tust, is a wonderful and terrible ſea-monſter, which extremely deſerves to be taken notice of by thoſe who are curious to look into the extraordinary works of the Great Creator. But I muſt firſt give the reader proper authorities of its real exiſtence, before I treat of its nature and properties. This creature, particularly in the North-sea, continually keeps himself in the bottom of the sea, excepting in the months of July or August, which is their spawning time, and they then come to the surface in calm weather, but plunge into the water again as soon as the wind raises the least wave.

In all my enquiries about this affair, I have hardly spoke with any intelligent person, born in the manor of Nordland, who was not able to give a pertinent answer, and strong assurances of the existence of this fish, and some of our North traders, that come here every year with their merchandize, think it a very strange question, when they are seriously asked, whether there be any such creature, they think it as ridiculous as if the question was put to them, whether there be such fish as eel or cod.

Last winter I fell by chance in conversation on this subject with captain Lawrence de Ferry, now commander in this place, who said that he had doubted a great while, whether there was any such creature, till he had an opportunity of being fully convinced, by ocular demonstration, in the year 1746. Though I had nothing material to object, still he was pleased, as a farther confirmation of what he advanced, to bring before the magistrates, at a late sessions in the city of Bergen, two sea-faring men, who were with him in the boat when he shot one of these monsters, and saw the snake, as well as the blood that discoloured the water. What the said men deposed upon oath in court, may be seen by the following instrument; the original was sent me, and I think it deserves to be printed at large. It runs thus.

"His majesty's chief advocate in Bergen, Albert Christian Dass, the recorder, Hans Christian Gartner, John Cl[illegible]es, Oliver Simensen, Oliver Brinchmand, George Konig for Conrad de Lange, Matthias Gram for Elias Peter Tucksen, Claus Natler for Didrick Hasslop, Jochum Fogh for Henry Hiort, and George Wiers for Hans Christian Byssing, sworn burghers and jury men, give evidence, that in the year of our Lord 1751, on the twenty-second day of February, at a sessions of justice in this city of Bergen, the procurator John Reutz appeared, and presented a letter which had been delivered to him that day, from the honourable Lawrence de Ferry, captain in the navy, and first pilot, dated the preceding day, Feb. 21, wherein he desires the said procurator to procure him written copies of the respective depositions, attested properly upon oath, relating to the before mentioned affair, and what there happened, and the said procurator, now present, for that purpose, humbly begs, that two men, namely, Nicholas Peterson Kopper, and Nicholas Nicholson Anglewigen, inhabitants of this city, may be admitted to make oath, that every particular set forth in the aforesaid letter is true, which deposition he desires may be entered in the act of that sessions. This letter was accordingly read to the said deponents, and is as follows.

Mr John Reutz,

The latter end of August, in the year 1746, as I was on a voyage, in my return from Trundhiem, in a very calm and hot day, having a mind to put in at Molde, it happened, that when we were arrived with my vessel within six English miles of the aforesaid Molde, being at a place called Jule-Næss, as I was reading in a book, I heard a kind of a murmuring voice from amongst the men at the oars, who were eight in number, and observed that the man at the helm kept off from the land. Upon this I enquired what was the matter, and was informed that there was a sea-snake before us. I then ordered the man at the helm to keep to the land again, and to come up with this crea-

creature, of which I had heard ſo many ſtories. Though the fellows were under ſome apprehenſions, they were obliged to obey my orders In the mean time this ſea-ſnake paſſed by us, and we were obliged to tack the veſſel about, in order to get nearer to it As the ſnake ſwam faſter than we could row, I took my gun, that was ready charged, and fired at it on this he immediately plunged under the water We rowed to the place where it ſunk down (which in the calm might be eaſily obſerved) and lay upon our oars, thinking it would come up again to the ſurface however, it did not When the ſnake plunged down, the water appeared thick and red, perhaps ſome of the ſhot might wound it, the diſtance being very little The head of this ſnake, which it held more than two feet above the ſurface of the water, reſembled that of a horſe. It was of a greyiſh colour, and the mouth was quite black, and very large It had black eyes, and a long white mane, that hung down from the neck to the ſurface of the water Beſides the head and neck, we ſaw ſeven or eight folds or coils of this ſnake, which were very thick, and, as far as we could gueſs, there was about a fathom diſtance between each fold I related this affair in a certain company, where there was a perſon of diſtinction preſent, who deſired that I would communicate to him an authentic detail of all that happened, and for this reaſon two of my ſailors, who were preſent at the ſame time and place when I ſaw this monſter, namely, Nicholas Pederſen Kopper, and Nicholas Nicholſon Anglewigen, ſhall appear in court, to declare on oath the truth of every particular herein ſet forth, and I deſire the favour of an atteſted copy of the ſaid deſcriptions

I remain, Sir, your obliged ſervant,

Bergen, Feb. 21, 1751.

L. de FERRY

After this the before-named witneſſes gave their corporal oaths, and with their finger held up according to law, witneſſed and confirmed the aforeſaid letter or declaration. and every particular ſet forth therein, to be ſtrictly true. A copy of the ſaid atteſtation was made out for the ſaid procurator Reutz, and granted by the recorder

That this was tranſacted in our court of juſtice, we confirm with our hands and ſeals. Actum Bergis, die & loco, ut ſupra

A C Dass. (L S) H C G[illegible]rt[illegible]er &c. (L S)

Governor Benſtrup affirms, that he ſaw the ſame creature a few years ago, and that he drew a ſketch of the ſea ſnake, which I wiſh I had to communicate to the public I have however inſerted a draught that I was favoured with by the before-mentioned clergyman, Mr Hans Strom, which he cauſed to be carefully made, under his own inſpection This agrees in every particular with the deſcription of this monſter, given by two of his neighbours at Herroe, namely Meſſ Reutz and Tuchſen, and of which they have been eye-witneſſes. I might mention to the ſame purpoſe many more perſons of equal credit and reputation Another drawing alſo, which appears more diſtinct with regard to the form of this creature, was taken from the Reverend Mr Egede's journal of the Greenland miſſion, where the account ſtands thus in p 6. " On the 6th of July, 1734, there appeared a very large and frightful ſea-monſter, which raiſed itſelf up ſo high out of the water, that its head reached above our main top It had a long ſharp ſnout, and ſpouted water like a whale, and very broad paws The body ſeemed to be covered with ſcales, and the ſkin was uneven and wrinkled, and the lower part was formed like a ſnake

After ſome time the creature plunged backwards into the water, and then turned its tail up above the ſurface a [illegible] whole

whole ſhip's length from the head. The following evening we had very bad weather." So far Mr Egede The drawing annexed gives me the greateſt reaſon to conclude, (what by other accounts I have thought probable) that there are ſea-ſnakes, like other fiſh, of different ſorts That which Mr Egede ſaw, and probably all thoſe who ſailed with him, had under its body two flaps, or perhaps two broad fins the head was longer, and the body thicker, but much ſhorter than thoſe ſea ſnakes, of which I have had the moſt confident accounts Though one cannot have an opportunity of taking the exact dimenſions of this creature, yet all that have ſeen it are unanimous in affirming, as far as they can judge at a diſtance, it appears to be of the length of a cable, i e 100 fathoms, or 600 Engliſh feet, that it lies on the ſurface of the water, (when it is very calm) in many folds, and that there are in a line with the head, ſome ſmall parts of the back to be ſeen above the ſurface of the water when it moves or bends These at a diſtance appear like ſo many caſks or hogſheads floating in a line, with a conſiderable diſtance between each of them Mr Tuchſen of Herroe, whom I mentioned above, is the only perſon, of the many correſpondents I have, that informs me he has obſerved the differences between the body and the tail of this creature as to thickneſs

It appears that this creature does not, like the Eel or Landſnake, taper gradually to a point, but the body, which looks to be as big as two hogſheads, grows remarkably ſmall at once juſt where the tail begins The head in all the kinds has a high and broad forehead, but in ſome a pointed ſnout, though in others that is flat, like that of a cow or horſe, with large noſtrils, and ſeveral [illegible] hairs ſtanding out on each ſide like whiſkers

It is ſuppoſed that the Sea-ſnakes have a very quick ſmell [illegible] may conclude from this, that they are obſerved to fly from the ſmell of caſtor Upon this account thoſe that go out on Stor Eggen to fiſh in the ſummer, always provide themſelves with this medicine They add, that the eyes of this creature are very large, and of a blue colour, and look like a couple of bright pewter plates The whole animal is of a dark brown colour, but it is ſpeckled and variegated with the light ſtreaks or ſpots, that ſhine like tortoiſe-ſhell It is of a darker hue about the eyes and mouth than elſewhere, and appears in that part a good deal like thoſe horſes, which we call Moors-heads

I do not find by any of my correſpondents, that the ſpout the water out of their noſtrils like the Whale only in that one inſtance related by Mr Egede, as mentioned above but when it approaches, it puts the water in great agitation, and makes it run like the current at a mill Thoſe on our coaſt differ likewiſe from the Greenland Sea-ſnakes, with regard to the ſkin, which is as ſmooth as glaſs, and has not the leaſt wrinkle, but about the neck, where there is a kind of mane, which looks like a parcel of ſea weeds hanging down to the water Some ſay it annually ſheds its ſkin like the Land-ſnake, and it is affirmed that a few years ſince there was to be ſeen at Kopperwiig, a cover for a table made of the ſkin of one of theſe ſnakes This raiſed my curioſity to know the truth, and accordingly I wrote thither for proper information, deſiring the favour of a ſlip of it, by way of ſpecimen, but it ſeems there was no ſuch thing, at leaſt not at that time beſides, a man that came from the place told me he had never heard any thing of it This perſon however informed me, that in the year 1720 a Sea ſnake had lain a whole week in a creek near that place, that it came there at high water through a narrow channel, about ſeven or eight feet broad, but went away, after

ter lying there a whole week, as mentioned above, and left behind it a ſkin, which this man, whoſe name is Thorlack Thorlackſen, declares he ſaw and handled. This ſkin lay with one end under water in the creek, and therefore, how long it was nobody could tell. It ſeems the creek within that channel is ſeveral fathoms deep, and it lay ſtretched out a great way; but the other end of the ſlouth had been driven aſhore by the tide, where it lay a long time, for every body to examine. He ſaid it did not ſeem fit to make a covering for a table, unleſs it had been properly dreſſed, or ſome other way prepared for that purpoſe: for it was not hard and compact, like a ſkin, but rather of a ſoft and ſlimy conſiſtence. Even the body itſelf is ſaid to be of the ſame nature, as I am informed by thoſe who, by accident, once caught a young one, and laid it upon the deck of the ſhip. It died inſtantly, though no-body dared to go near it even then, till they were obliged to throw it overboard, by the inſupportable ſtink which was cauſed by the ſoft and viſcid ſlime, to which it was at length diſſolved by the action of the wind. It ſeems the wind is ſo deſtructive to this creature, that, as has been obſerved before, it is never ſeen on the ſurface of the water, but in the greateſt calm, and the leaſt guſt of wind drives it immediately to the bottom again. One of theſe Sea-ſnakes was ſeen at Amunds Vaagen, in Norfiord, ſome years ago. It came in between the rocks, probably at high water, and died there. It was obſerved that the carcaſe occaſioned an intolerable ſtench for a long time. It is ſaid the ſame alſo happened at the iſland of Karmen, and in ſeveral other places. I wiſh that, on ſuch opportunities, ſomebody had examined the creature carefully, to ſee whether it had a ſtrong back bone, which ſeems neceſſary to ſupport ſuch a length.

The Shark kind, which are alſo of the cartilaginous claſs, and without other bones, yet have a backbone, though that is but very ſlender, even in the largeſt ſpecies, which are often twenty feet in length. The Sea-ſnake ſeems alſo to me, like the Shark, Eel, and Whale-kind, viviparous. It appears that they ſeek their mates at a certain time of the year, in order, as it is ſaid, to couple. For this reaſon it is ſuppoſed they follow ſhips and boats at thoſe times, which probably appear to them to be creatures of their own kind. If this, which I have from the accounts of our ſea-faring people be true, then I conclude they are miſtaken, who ſuppoſe that the Sea-ſnake does not breed in the ſea, but on dry land; and that it lives in rocks and woods, till it can no longer be concealed, and then betakes itſelf to rivers, in order to get into the ſea. There are ſome that pretend they have ſeen this.

I return again to the Sea-ſnake, properly ſo called, or the ſerpent of the ocean, and particularly to the moſt intereſting inquiry concerning them, which is, whether they do mankind any injury? And in what manner they may hurt the human ſpecies? Arndt Bernſen, in his account of the fertility of Denmark and Norway, p. 308, affirms that they do; and ſays, that the Sea ſnake, as well as the Trold-whale, often ſinks both men and boats. I have not heard any account of ſuch an accident hereabouts, that might be depended upon; but the North traders inform me of what has frequently happened with them, namely, that the Sea ſnake has raiſed itſelf up, and thrown itſelf acroſs a boat, and ſometimes even acroſs a veſſel of ſome hundred tons burden, and by its weight has ſunk it down to the bottom. One of the aforeſaid North traders, who ſays that he has been near enough to ſome of theſe Sea-ſnakes (alive) to feel their ſmooth ſkin, [illegible] that ſometimes they

take

raise up their frightful heads, and snap a man out of a boat, without hurting the rest but I will not affirm this for a truth, because it is not certain that they are a fish of prey Yet this, and their enmity to mankind, can be no more determined, than that of the Land-snake, by the words of the prophet Amos, Cap. ix v 3 " And though they be hid from my sight in the bottom of the sea, thence will I command the serpent, and he shall bite them "

It is said that they sometimes fling themselves in a wide circle round a boat, so that the men are surrounded on all sides This Snake, I observed before, generally appears on the water in folds or coils, and the fishermen, from a known custom in that case, never row towards the openings, or those places where the body is not seen, but is concealed under the water, if they did, the snake would raise itself up, and overset the boat. On the contrary, they row full against the highest part that is visible, which makes the snake immediately dive, and thus they are released from their fears This is their method when they cannot avoid them but when they see one of these creatures at a distance, they row away with all their might (by which they sometimes injure their health) towards the shore, or into a creek, where it cannot follow them

When they are far from land it would be in vain to attempt to row away from them, for these creatures shoot through the water like an arrow out of a bow, seeking constantly the coldest places In this case they put the former method in execution, or lie upon their oars, and throws any thing that comes to hand at them. If it be but a scuttle, or any light thing, so they be touched, they generally plunge into the water, or take another course Of late our fishermen have found the way, in the warm summer months, of providing themselves with castor, which they always carry with them when they go far out to sea they shut it up in a hole in the stern, and if at any time they are particularly apprehensive of meeting with the sea-snake, they throw a little of it overboard; for by frequent experience they know of a certainty, that it always avoids this drug Luke Debes tells us, in his *Færoa reserata*, p 167, that in that country also they use it with the same success, as the best defence against the Trold whale, a fish that likewise often oversets boats, but which has a great aversion to castor and shavings of juniper wood These they throw out to him therefore when in danger The author, just cited also says, that various experiments confirm this singular phenomenon, that if any man has castor about him when in the water, he sinks instantly to the bottom like a stone, though he be ever so good a swimmer For the truth of this he relies upon the testimony of Thom Bartholin in Centur. II Histor Anatom Hist 17 p 201.

An eminent apothecary here has informed me, that, instead of castor, our fishermen provide themselves with nothing but *assa fœtida*, by way of defence against the hurtful sea animals for if what they carry have but a strong smell, it has the same effect upon those sea snakes, &c besides, *assa fœtida* comes at a lower price than castor

In the remote parts of Norway, according to some accounts, people have been poisoned with the excrements of the sea serpent, which are often seen here, especially in Nordland, in the summer months, floating on the water like a fat slime. This viscid matter is supposed by our fishermen to be somewhat vomited up by them, or else their sperm, or some other humour If a fisherman finds this matter near his net, and inadvertently let any of it touch his hand, it will occasion a painful swelling and inflammation, which has often

often proved so dangerous as to require an amputation of the limb.

Ni[l] prodest quod non lædere possit idem

Sir, Le[i]gh, Feb 2, 1771.

A Few years ago, three lads, apprentices to a weaver in Spitalfields, upon a little indisposition, besought their mistress to procure them some purges

A sailor happening unluckily to be at her house at the time, she asked him what sort she should give them. He answered, gamboge, as was commonly used on board of ships, and cured all ills

Accordingly, on Sunday morning (to save a day) she indiscreetly gave a piece to every one, by guess only, which soon worked so violently, as to dispatch the two youngest, even before people returned from church

The eldest, and stoutest, nearly out of his time, was ordered to run into the garden, and walk briskly about, in order, as they thought, for the rough physic to work off the quicker, but finding himself unable to hold out any longer, and offering to enter the house again, he sudden ly fell down dead on the threshold of the door

They were all three conveyed in a hearse, and interred together, at the same time, in Stepney church-yard

A similar accident happened in our hundred of Rochford, told me last week by an eye witness of the fact A dredger's wife asked her near neighbour what she should purge her husband's two apprentices with, who told her, with as much gamboge, in powder, as could lie on a shilling on a Sunday morning too she gave the same dose to both, one being about fourteen years of age, and weakly, and the other twenty

My informer left them in violent [illegible]erably, both upwards and [illegible] church, and [illegible]d to find them laying out the youngest. ——The eldest, from his superior strength, held it out, narrowly escaping death, but not without a Palsy, succeeding on the extremities, which took away the use of his limbs. He was sent to the hospital, where he slowly recovered their motion by degrees, and at present is alive and well

Hoffman, and some others, condemn this medicine, as acting with too much violence, and occasioning dangerous hypercatharses, whilst others are of a contrary opinion.—— Geoffroy seems particularly fond of it, and informs us that he has frequently given it from two to four grains, without its proving at all emetic, that from four to eight grains it both vomits and purges with violence; that its operation is soon over; and that if exhibited in a liquid form, and sufficiently diluted, it stands not in need of any corrector; that in the form of a bolus, or pill, it is (by its delay) most apt to prove emetic, but very rarely has this effect, if joined with sweet mercury. He nevertheless cautions against its use, where the patient can't easily bear vomiting

I mention such melancholy accidents by way of precaution, to prevent the like fatal effects for the future, and to advise both patient and prescriber never to use such drastic purges, without good advice, and proper directions

I have indeed, upon certain occasions, as for incipient dropsies, ordered it to even ten or twelve grains for a dose, but it was to robust bodies only, who could bear great shaking ---not else. It is certainly an excellent drug in some difficult cases, when used with judgment, but a dangerous medicine in the hands of the ignorant and unskilful---the very best medicines always becoming the very worst when misused

Your's, &c

J COOK

A Letter

A Letter of the late Reverend Mr STERNE

THE firſt time I have dipped my pen into the ink-horn for this week paſt, is to write to you, and to thank you moſt ſincerely for your kind epiſtle!—Will this be a ſufficient apology for my letting it lie ten days upon my table without anſwering it —I truſt it will,—I am ſure my own feelings tell me ſo,—becauſe I feel it to be impoſſible for me to do any thing that is ungracious towards you It is not every hour or day or week of a man's life that is a fit ſeaſon for the duties of friendſhip —ſentiment is not always at hand,—folly and pride, and what is called buſineſs, oftentimes keep it at a diſtance,—and without ſentiment what is friendſhip!—a name!—a ſhadow!—But to prevent a miſapplication of all this (though why ſhould I fear it from ſo kind and gentle a ſpirit as yours?) you muſt know, that by the careleſſneſs of my Curate, or his wife, or his maid, or ſome one within his gates, the parſonage houſe at ——— was about a fortnight ago burnt to the ground, with the furniture which belonged to me, and a pretty good collection of books,—the loſs about 350l.---The poor man with his wife took the wings of the next morning and fled away ---This has given me real vexation,---for ſo much was my pity and eſteem for him, that as ſoon as I heard of the diſaſter, I ſent to deſire he would come and take his abode with me, till another habitation was ready to receive him, but he was gone, and, as I have been told, through fear of my perſecution ---Heavens! how little did he know me, to ſuppoſe that I was among the number of thoſe wretches, who heap misfortune upon misfortune, and when the load is almoſt inſupportable, ſtill add to the weight —God, who reads my heart, knows it to be true, that I wiſh rather to ſhare than to encreaſe the burden of the miſerable,---to dry up, inſtead of adding a ſingle drop to the ſtream of ſorrow ---As for the dirty traſh of this world, I regard it not,---the loſs of it does not coſt me a ſigh,---for after all, I may ſay with the Spaniſh Captain, that I am as good a gentleman as the King, only not quite ſo rich.---But to the point ---

Shall I expect you here this ſummer?---I much wiſh that you may make it convenient to gratify me in a viſit for a few weeks I will give you a roaſt fowl for your dinner, and a clean table-cloth every day, and tell you a ſtory by way of deſart.--- In the heat of the day we will ſit in the ſhade, and in the evening, the faireſt of all the milk-maids who paſs by my gate, ſhall wave a garland for you

—If I ſhould be ſo unfortunate as not to ſee you here, do contrive to meet me in London the beginning of October ---I ſhall ſtay there about a fortnight, and then ſeek a kinder climate!---This plaguy cough of mine ſeems to gain ground, and will bring me at laſt to my grave, in ſpite of all I can do, but while I have ſtrength enough to run away from it, I will!---I have been wreſtling with it for theſe twenty years paſt, and what with laughter and good ſpirits have prevented its giving me a fall but my antagoniſt preſſes cloſer than ever upon me, and I have nothing left on my ſide but another journey abroad!---A propos,---are you for a ſcheme of that ſort?---If not,---perhaps you will be ſo good as to accompany me as far as Dover, that we may laugh together upon the beach, to put Neptune in good humour, before I embark ---God bleſs you ---Adieu

A CRITIQUE *on the new Comedy of the* WEST INDIAN.

WHENEVER the public has given such marks of its approbation to any dramatic performance, as it has lately done to the Comedy of the West-Indian, it is the duty of every critical writer, in justice to that Public, the Author, and himself, to consider carefully the merits and demerits of the play in question, before he shall venture to contradict, or even join the applause of crowded theatres. I will grant that the Public may, and has been misled in many instances, and that it is the duty of the true critic to point out the errors it has run into, for the general good; but then, the public judgment should not be appealed from too rashly, nor an author's property and reputation attacked wantonly or malevolently.

I preface thus much in defence of critical decency, as it is now become the mode to hurry undigested panegyric or animadversion into News-Papers and Magazines upon plays, not only before they are printed, and consequently before they are read, but even before they are well seen. I need not prove the injustice of such a proceeding, nor point out the particular places where such instances of human weakness and malice are to be found. I shall content myself to speak fairly and impartially my own sentiments, and shall be ready to change them if a better judge of these matters will as fairly and impartially convince me of my errors.

Having often attended the representation of this new comedy before the publication of it, I confess that I never received more pleasure from any theatrical performance, nor did I find, by a calm perusal of the same piece in my closet, that the actors had, by their art and cunning, imposed counters upon me for sterling money.

February, 1771.

As I am now as well qualified to give my reasons for this opinion as I ever can be, I only beg that your readers will be as candid as I am, and consider what a plain impartial man has to say for and against the present object of their praise and admiration.

The West-Indian is of that species of comedy, which I think all writers upon the drama agree to place in the first class, viz. a groupe of characters concerned in an interesting plot. --The characters are strong, and of that kind which rarely sink into low humour, and never into farce. It is likewise a comedy of sentiment, in the best sense of the term; for the sentiments are so incorporated with the character, that they appear to be every person's natural language. I will endeavour, by a familiar instance, to shew the difference between characteristic sentiment, and that which is too commonly made use of in modern comedies.---The first is a rich embroidery, interwoven, as it were, with the stuff it adorns, and cannot be removed from it; the other is a clumsy, tasteless, ill-suited Appliquée, and may be taken off, or put upon, any other cloth or colour, but can never appear of a piece with any of them.-- For example, nothing has been more hacked in our trageaies and comedies, than the praise of liberty; and it cannot indeed be too often inculcated, if it is brought upon the stage characteristically.

At the entrance of the young West-Indian, he gives an account of the bustle and scuffle he had at his landing with the mob; upon which Stockwell says, "Well, Mr Belcour, 'tis a rough sample you have had of my countrymen's spirit; but I trust you will not think the worse of them for it."

"*Belcour.* Not at all, not at all; I like 'em the better. were I only a visitor, I might perhaps wish them a little more tractable; but as a fellow

low

ow subject, and a sharer in the freedom, I applaud their spirit, though I feel the effects in every bone of my skin."

What can be more easy, natural, and spirited than this answer? I could give many instances of the characteristic [illegible] in Belcour, but I took the first that occurred, as a pattern of the best kind of dramatic embroidery. Dudley, [illegible] an old officer, is as full of sentiment as virtue, and yet I will answer, that no spectator or reader has thought him either formal or dull---And why? Because his sentiments are characteristic. I know no character has more sentiment than that excellent one of Major O'Flaherty, and yet his thoughts are so adapted to his turn of mind and expression, that you laugh at in him, what you would admire in another person. The famous line in Terence,

Homo sum, humani nihil a me alienum puto,

(thus excellently translated by Colman---

"I am a man, and feel for all mankind.)

is reported to have had an astonishing effect upon a Roman audience: nor had the following noble trait of character less effect on an English one, when spoken by the Major.---"I suspect the old Lady has not been over generous to poor Dudley, I'll [illegible] give her a little touch upon that: upon my soul I know but one excuse a person can have for giving nothing, and that is, like myself, having nothing to give."

I will venture to affirm, that the following [illegible] from the last scene in the 2d act between Lady Rusport and the Irish Major, will give a [illegible] pleasure to a generous [illegible] of laughter [illegible] [illegible] [illegible]

"*Lady Rusport*. Would you believe it, Major O'Flaherty, it was but this morning he sent a begging to me for money, to fit him out upon some wild goose expedition to the coast of Africa, I know not where.

"*O'Flaherty*. Well, you sent him what he wanted?

"*Lady Rusport*. I sent him what he deserved, a flat refusal.

"*O'Flaherty*. You refused him!

"*Lady Rusport*. Most undoubtedly.

"*O'Flaherty*. You sent him nothing?

"*Lady Rusport*. Not a shilling.

"*O'Flaherty*. Good morning to you---Your servant---[going.

"*Lady Rusport*. Hey day! What ails the man? Where are you going?

"*O'Flaherty*. Out of your house, before the roof falls on my head---to poor Dudley, to share the little modicum that thirty years hard service has left me; I wish it was more, for his sake.

"*Lady Rusport*. Very well, Sir, take your course, I shan't attempt to stop you, I shall survive it; it will not break my heart if I never see you more.

"*O'Flaherty*. Break your heart! No, o' my conscience, will it not---You preach, and you pray, and you turn up your eyes, and all the while you're as hard-hearted as a Hyena---a Hyena, truly! By my soul, there isn't in the whole creation so savage an animal as a human creature without pity.---[Exit."

Give me leave to stop the warmth of my regard for this personage, and, without offence to the author, make an objection to the major's boasting of his five wives; I know it will be said, that it is qualified by the [illegible] but I say, it is not of a piece with the Major's principles, to [illegible] of his women like a young military coxcomb, nor make a joke of [illegible] [illegible], and leaving them---

[illegible]

There

There are two characters in this comedy which have always given me great delight, from their novelty and nature, I mean the young lovers--- Miss Rusport being in love with a worthy young officer of no fortune, declares her passion in a noble, but delicate, manner, and raises her character by a behaviour which would sink it, were the circumstances reverted. Young Dudley, on the other hand, from a delicate consciousness of his want of fortune, stifles the warm impulse of his passion for Miss Rusport, and appears cool to her noble generous declarations. The moment it is known that he has got a fortune, equal if not superior to her's, she grows reserved, and he is all transport and affection. There is something so original and so pleasing in the management and conduct of these two characters, that I pronounce them the production of a most elegant mind, and formed to succeed in that very dangerous but honourable employment, of entertaining the public.

I have now gone through with my first task of laying before your readers the characters, and what I mean by the characteristic sentiments of the comedy. I have not said any thing of two of the principal personages in the Drama, Mr Stockwell and lady Rusport, the first makes a reputable figure in the drama, but has nothing particularly to mark him from many other fathers upon the stage; the part is well written, and most worthily employed. Lady Rusport, who is most artfully introduced as a contrast to her daughter in-law, and gives that variety which is required to keep up the spirit of the Drama, may have some resemblance to other characters upon the stage, but the author, in his manner of employing her, has made her his own. The subordinate parts of Mr and Mrs Fulmer have their merit, they are literally procurers to the audience, and bring about every circumstance and situation of distress and pleasure without them, the amiable miss Dudley had not passed for her brother's mistress, nor the spirit, passion, generosity, and frailty of Belcour appeared in such full perfection. The circumstance of the jewels, the great struggle between passion and honour, the mistakes of young Dudley, miss Dudley, Belcour, and miss Rusport, are all owing to this worthy couple, who likewise make no inconsiderable figure, though they are the inferior engines of the Drama.

I shall next consider the foundation, conduct, and unravelling of the plot, its merits and defects, &c and hope I shall have something to say upon the terms *probability* and *possibility*, which may not be disagreeable to your readers, if it should prove as profitable and entertaining as I intend it shall be new.

JUNIUS *on the late Negotiations with Spain*

IF we recollect in what manner the king's friends have been constantly employed, we shall have no reason to be surprised at any condition of disgrace, to which the once respected name of Englishman may be degraded. His Majesty has no cares, but such as concern the laws and constitution of this country. In his royal breast there is no room left for resentment, no place for hostile sentiments against the natural enemies of his crown. The system of government is uniform ---Violence and oppression at home can only be supported by treachery and submission abroad. When the civil rights of the people are daringly invaded on one side, what have we to expect, but that their political rights should be deserted and betrayed, in the same proportion, on the other? The plan of domestic policy, which has been invariably pursued, from the moment of his present majesty's accession, engrosses all the attention of his

his servants. They know that the security of their places depends upon their maintaining, at any hazard, the secret system of the closet. A foreign war might embarrass, an unfavourable event might ruin the minister, and defeat the deep laid scheme of policy, to which he and his associates owe their employments. Rather than suffer the execution of that scheme to be delayed or interrupted, the king has been advised to make a public surrender, a solemn sacrifice, in the face of all Europe, not only of the interests of his subjects, but of his own personal reputation, and of the dignity of that crown, which his predecessors have worn with honour. These are strong terms, Sir, but they are supported by fact and argument.

The king of Great Britain had been, for some years in possession of an island, to which, as the ministry themselves have repeatedly asserted, the Spaniards had no claim of right. The importance of the place is not in question. If it were, a better judgment might be formed of it from the opinions of lord Anson and lord Egmont, and from the anxiety of the Spaniards, than from any fallacious insinuations thrown out by men, whose interest it is to undervalue that property which they are determined to relinquish. [illegible] ... courts. [illegible] ... The [illegible] ... appears directly to the [illegible] ... The [illegible] ... [illegible]

ing our people to depart. At last a military force appears, and compels the garrison to surrender. A formal capitulation ensues, and his majesty's ship, which might at least have been permitted to bring home his troops immediately, is detained in port twenty days, and her rudder forcibly taken away. This train of facts carries no appearance of the rashness or violence of a Spanish governor. On the contrary, the whole plan seems to have been formed and executed, in consequence of deliberate orders, and a regular instruction from the Spanish court. Mr Buccarelli is not a pirate, nor has he been treated as such by those who employed him. I feel for the honour of a gentleman, when I affirm that our king owes him a signal reparation.---Where will the humiliations of this country end!---A king of Great Britain, not contented with placing himself upon a level with a Spanish governor, descends so low as to do a notorious injustice to that governor. As a salvo for his own reputation, he has been advised to traduce the character of a brave officer, and to treat him as a common robber, when he knew with certainty that Mr Buccarelli had acted in obedience to his orders, and had done no more than his duty. Thus it happens, in private life, with a man [illegible] ... of honour. [illegible] ... equal orders [illegible] ... him.---Instead of [illegible] ... blow to the master [illegible] ... equally false and [illegible] ... character of the [illegible]

[illegible] recapitulation [illegible] ... introduce the consideration [illegible] ... speech, and the subsequent [illegible] ... of government [illegible] ... with which the [illegible] self, whenever it happened, must, in some degree, be dishonourable to [illegible]. There appears through the whole speech a guard and reserve in the choice of expression, which shews how careful the ministry were not to embarrass their future conduct by any firm or spirited declaration from the throne. When all hopes of peace are lost, his majesty tells his parliament, that he is preparing, – not for barbarous war, but (with all his mother's softness) 'for a different situation.' — It would indeed be happy for this country, if the lady I speak of were obliged to prepare herself for a different situation. — An open hostility, authorized by the catholic king, is called 'an act of a governor.' This act, to avoid the mention of a regular siege and surrender, passes under the piratical description of 'seizing by force,' and the thing taken is described, not as a part of the king's territory or proper dominion, but merely as a 'possession,' a word expressly chosen in contradistinction to, and exclusion of, the idea of 'right,' and to prepare us for a future surrender both of the right and of the possession. Yet this speech, Sir, cautious and equivocal as it is, cannot, by any sophistry, be accommodated to the measures which have since been adopted. It seemed to promise, that whatever might be given up by secret stipulation, some care would be taken to save appearances to the public. The event shews us, that, to depart, in the minutest article, from the nicety and strictness of punctilio, is as dangerous to national honour, as to female virtue. The woman, who admits of one familiarity, seldom knows where to stop, or what to refuse; and when the counsels of a great country give way in a single instance — [illegible] they are inclined to [illegible] accelerates the [illegible] of the [illegible]. The mi[illegible] [illegible] [illegible] [illegible] cede to such an accommodation, as they have since advised their master to accept of.

The king says, 'The honour of my crown and the rights of my people are deeply affected.' The Spaniard, in his reply, says, 'I give you no satisfaction, but I adhere to my claim of prior right, reserving the assertion of it for a more favourable opportunity.'

The speech says, 'I made an immediate demand of satisfaction, and, if that fail, I am prepared to do myself justice.' This immediate demand must have been sent to Madrid on the 12th of September, or in a few days after. It was certainly refused, or evaded, and the king has not done himself justice. — When the first magistrate speaks to the nation, some care should be taken of his apparent veracity.

The speech proceeds to say, 'I shall not discontinue my preparations, until I have received proper reparation for the injury.' If this assurance may be relied on, what an enormous expence is entailed, *sine die*, upon this unhappy country! Restitution of a possession, and reparation of an injury, are as different in substance, as they are in language. The very act of restitution may [illegible] in [illegible] palpable [illegible] aggravation of the injury. A man of spirit does not measure the degree of an injury by the mere positive damage he has sustained. He considers the principle on which it is founded; he resents the superiority asserted over him; and rejects with indignation the claim of right, which his adversary endeavours to establish, and would force him to acknowledge.

The motives on which the catholic king makes the restitution, are, if possible, more insolent and disgraceful to our sovereign than even the declaratory condition annexed to it. After taking four months to consider [illegible] [illegible] expedition was undertaken

dertaken by his own orders or not, he condescends to disavow the enterprize, and restore the island ---not from any regard to justice, --- not from any regard he bears to his Britannic majesty, but merely from the persuasion in which he is of the pacific sentiments of the king of Great Britain?---At this rate, if our king had discovered the spirit of a man,--if he had made a peremptory demand of satisfaction, the king of Spain would have given him a peremptory refusal. But why this unseasonable, this ridiculous mention of the king of Great Britain's pacific intentions? Have they ever been in question? Was he the aggressor? Does he attack foreign powers without provocation? Does he even resist when he is insulted? No, Sir, if any ideas of strife or hostility have entered his royal mind, they have a very different direction. The enemies of England have nothing to fear from them.

After all, Sir, to what kind of disavowal has the king of Spain at last consented? Supposing it made in proper time, it should have been accompanied with instant restitution; and, if Mr. Buccarelli acted without orders, he deserved death. Now, Sir, instead of immediate restitution, we have four months negotiation, and the officer, whose act is disavowed, returns to court, and is loaded with honours.

If the actual situation of Europe be considered, the treachery of the king's servants, particularly of lord North, who takes the whole upon himself, will appear in the strongest colours of aggravation. Our allies were masters of the Mediterranean. The king of France's present aversion from war, and the distraction of his affairs, are notorious. He is now in a state of war with his people. In vain did the Catholic king solicit him to take part in the quarrel against us. His finances were in the last disorder, and it was probable that his troops might find sufficient employment at home. In these circumstances, we might have dictated the law to Spain. There are no terms, to which she might not have been compelled to submit. At the worst, a war with Spain alone carries the fairest promise of advantage. One good effect at least would have been immediately produced by it. The desertion of France would have irritated her ally, and in all probability have dissolved the family compact. The scene is now fatally changed. The advantage is thrown away,-- the most favourable opportunity is lost. Hereafter we shall know the value of it. When the French king is reconciled to his subjects,--when Spain has compleated her preparations---when the collected strength of the House of Bourbon attacks us at once, the king himself will be able to determine upon the wisdom or imprudence of his present conduct. As far as the probability of argument extends, we may safely pronounce, that a conjecture, which threatens the very being of this country, has been wilfully prepared and forwarded by our own ministry. How far the people may be animated to resistance under the present administration, I know not; but this I know with certainty, that, under the present administration, or if any thing like it should continue, it is of very little moment whether we are a conquered nation or not.

Having travelled thus far in the high road of matter of fact, I may now be permitted to wander a little into the field of imagination. Let us banish from our minds the persuasion that these events have really happened in the reign of the best of princes. Let us consider them as nothing more than the materials of a fable, in which we may conceive the sovereign of some other country to be concerned. I mean to violate all the laws of probability, when I suppose that this imaginary king, after having voluntarily disgraced himself in the eyes of his subjects, might re-

tu

turn to a sense of his dishonour---that he might perceive the snare laid for him by his ministers, and feel a spark of shame kindling in his breast.---The part he must then be obliged to act, would overwhelm him with confusion. To his parliament he must say, 'I called you together to receive your advice, and have never asked your opinion.'---To the merchant,--'I have distressed your commerce; I have dragged your seamen out of your ships; I have loaded you with a grievous weight of insurances.'---To the land holder,---'I told you war was too probable, when I was determined to submit to any terms of accommodation; I extorted new taxes from you, before it was possible they could be wanted, and am now unable to account for the application of them.'---To the public creditor,---'I have delivered up your fortunes a prey to foreigners, and to the vilest of your fellow subjects.' Perhaps this repenting prince might conclude with one general acknowledgment to them all---'I have involved every rank of my subjects in anxiety and distress, and have nothing to offer you in return, but the certainty of national dishonour, an armed truce, and peace without security.'

If these accounts were settled, there would still remain an apology to be made to his navy, and to his army. To the first he would say, 'You were once the terror of the world. But go back to your harbours. A man dishonoured, as I am, has no use for your services.' It is not probable that he would appear again before his soldiers, even in the pacific ceremony of a review. But wherever he appeared, the humiliating confession would be extorted from him. 'I have received a blow, and had not spirit to resent it. I demanded satisfaction, and have accepted a declaration, in which the right to strike me again is asserted and confirmed.' His countenance at least would speak this language, and even his guards would blush for him.

But to return to our argument.---The ministry, it seems, are labouring to draw a line of distinction between the honour of the crown and the rights of the people. This new idea has yet been only started in discourse, for in effect both objects have been equally sacrificed. I neither understand the distinction, nor what use the ministry propose to make of it. The king's honour is that of his people. Their real honour and real interest are the same.---I am not contending for a vain punctilio. A clear unblemished character comprehends not only the integrity that will not offer, but the spirit that will not submit to an injury; and whether it belongs to an individual or to a community, it is the foundation of peace, of independence, and of safety. Private credit is wealth; public honour is security.---The feather that adorns the royal bird, supports his flight. Strip him of his plumage, and you fix him to the earth.

JUNIUS.

The Speeches made in the Great Assembly, on the 25th of January, on Mr. DOWD——WELL's *Motion, when the Spanish Declaration, and the Earl of Rochford's Acceptance of it, were read in a great Assembly.*

JER——H DYS——N *spoke.*

SIR,

IT appears to me that the K---g's Speech abstained with great propriety from touching on our right to the Island of Falkland, and confined itself solely to the assertion of its own honour, and the security of the people's rights, which in it were said to be deeply affected. This motion though it may seem at first to echo back the words delivered from the throne, is essentially different both in language and sense. In the latter the security

security of our rights, in the former, our [illegible] [illegible], are declared to be deeply affected. If then this motion passes the house in its present form, we [illegible] [illegible] language, but an opinion [illegible] those of his majesty [illegible] [illegible] that the right to [illegible] is vested in the crown of Great Britain, and not in that of Spain, and by that step we throw a reflection both on his majesty, and on the ministry: on his majesty, because he did not immediately and expressly assert our right; on the ministry, because they concluded the negotiation without establishing our right. Now I take this proceeding to be very injurious, because our right has not been yet proved.

I ought not however to be surprised, that these expressions should be contended for by opposition. They have been evidently chosen in order to convince the public, that the king and his ministers want steadiness in the support of the national interest. It was hoped that they would have passed unnoticed, and that they might have been quoted as [illegible] of irresolution in his majesty's council, and of the house's having condemned the ministers for not having obtained from Spain an express declaration in favour of our right to Falkland's Island.

But what if there should be no papers relative to the [illegible] [illegible] the ministers [illegible] [illegible] our right the [illegible] [illegible] [illegible]. What if the negotiation should have been [illegible] [illegible] [illegible] reparation for the affront [illegible] on the crown? In that case, this clause of the motion would be evidently absurd, because it would be impossible for the crown or ministers to comply with it. They could not produce what never existed ——— that this is the case, is, I am sure, more than probable, from the tenor and purport of the language, which the ministers have always [illegible] [illegible] in this house [illegible] [illegible] [illegible] place. What then would be the consequences of this demand? It might create unreasonable expectations among the people, and their representatives, and the disappointment might be turned greatly to the disadvantage of administration. The arts of faction might raise a clamour against them, by insinuating that, conscious of mismanagement, they had secreted the papers, in order to conceal their blunders from the prying eye of the public. This engine of discontent was played off against Walpole. With what justice, I will not say. But played off it was, and it proved of infinite prejudice to his cause. Why then should we not here apprehend the same stratagems, the same manœuvres of patriotic generalship? Is it because our modern sons of discontent always deal upon the square, and despise all trick and finesse? I fear their conduct, viewed without prejudice, will not justify so charitable a supposition. Some late instances clearly evince that the ruin of those who stand in their way to preferment, is with them a greater object than justice.

[illegible] D——g spoke next.

SIR,

WERE we even to suppose the [illegible] words of the clause, [illegible] which we have heard so many far fetched arguments, and ridiculous cavils, not to be these, which are found in the speech from the throne, yet I cannot see how they would prove detrimental to the ministry, or to any other set of men. The people always will, and do now put their own construction on their conduct. They do not wait for our decision in order to form their opinion. They think and judge for themselves, and they are very capable of thinking and judging rightly. Their voice has frequently been contrary to [illegible] [illegible] [illegible] [illegible] they were

were not ſuſpicious of its integrity, and they have often corrected its miſtakes. Recollect how they acted in the caſe of the Middleſex election, and confeſs that they are not puppets ſet in motion by your machinery. They attend to facts and the reaſon of things, and judge accordingly.

When the neceſſary papers are produced, they will give a verdict conformable to the evidence. Nor do I doubt but the miniſter's trained bands will be ſwayed in their determination, by the weightieſt arguments. The force of a golden Syllogiſm none can feel better.

Thus then it appears, that no bad conſequences are to be apprehended from the obnoxious words, as they now ſtand, even if we ſuppoſe them contrary to the expreſſions of his majeſty's ſpeech. Neither the people nor their repreſentatives, will entertain a better or worſe opinion of this convention. They will judge for themſelves, the people, the oppoſition, and the miniſterial dependents, being influenced by different motives.

Such is the ſtate of the caſe, when we conſider the motion in this point as diametrically oppoſite to the king's ſpeech. What then will it be, if they ſhould be found exactly to coincide? An alteration will not only be improper, but impoſſible. Now the fact is, that the words are the ſame. Not a ſyllable, not a ſingle letter is altered. Therefore, if they had in the king's ſpeech the meaning aſſigned by the noble lord, they will in the motion have the ſame. The ſame rules of grammar and explanation are applicable to them in the one caſe as in the other.

Why then all theſe cavils, all theſe obſtructions, raiſed againſt a meaſure that is ſo reaſonable, and even neceſſary? Do you mean, by an indirect attack, by a maſqued battery, to overturn what you dare not face upon fair ground [illegible] be [illegible] ſe [illegible] tention, I fear you will be diſappointed. Your ſtratagems will be counteracted, and your artifices expoſed. We penetrate your deſigns, and we will drag every *Guy Faux* into *open day*.

Colonel BAR---E *ſpoke next.*

SIR,

THERE are certain ſpeakers, who have the qualities of the Torpedo, who by their drowſy periods and droning accents, benumb the ſenſes, and produce all the apparent effects of a lethargy. As they make the houſe yawn, ſo they would lull it aſleep, were it not occaſionally rouſed by your *Hear him! hear Him!* Other orators there are, who reſemble the Scuttle-fiſh, who, if hard preſſed, jumble and confound every thing, and eſcape from their enemy in the obſcurity of their own chaos. In this ſpecies, I think, the laſt ſpeaker but one ought to be claſſed. He is a mere Scuttle-fiſh. What was before clear and evident, he perplexes and obſcures. Nor is he unaptly compared to a ſmoke jack, which, if ſurveyed, when it happens to be out of order, puzzles and blinds you with clouds of duſt and volumes of ſmoke. The motion was originally clear and diſtinct, and will be ſo ſtill, if he and his coadjutors ceaſe to involve it in darkneſs.

As to theſe ſtrange papers, which lie on your table, I do not now propoſe to enter into a minute diſcuſſion of them. But let others act as they will, I cannot contain my indignation. I wonder how the blood of Engliſhmen can be ſo cold and inanimate as not to take fire at the very firſt hearing of ſuch a diſgraceful compromiſe. For my own part, I am made up of more inflammable materials. I feel for the loſt honour of my country, and I muſt give vent to my paſſion, or burſt.

Where now, ye daſtardly miniſters, are all your confident aſſertions

 and

and your boaſt of preſerving inviolable the honour of the Britiſh crown and the rights of the Britiſh nation! Shame be upon you! After a negotiation of ſix months, and an expence of ſeveral millions, you have at laſt ſecured us——what? Not the right to the conteſted iſland, nor the whole iſland itſelf, but the bare poſſeſſion of Port Egmont in that iſland. May not Spain then renew her claim to-morrow, and reduce you to the very ſituation which you wiſhed to avoid? Certainly. What then have you gained by theſe TWO THINGS on your table? Any indemnification for your expence, any retaliation for the injury received? Not the leaſt of either. Well, ſince theſe eſſential points were relinquiſhed, has our honour been preſerved? On the contrary, it has been ſcandalouſly betrayed, though the quarrel was evidently a quarrel of honour, and not of intereſt, as the iſland could be of little real ſervice to England.

But how, you will aſk, like Nicodemus, can theſe things be? Were the miniſters ASLEEP, or MAD, or DRUNK? Well may you wonder, for the thing is as marvellous and incomprehenſible as the NEW BIRTH. It is ſo much out of nature, that it could never have happened if the public good had been, as it ought to be, the ſtandard of their conduct. But ſuch a leſſon is not taught in the political ſchool, where they have received their virtuous education. In that ſeminary they have learned to poſtpone every thing to their own intereſt, and to make the preſervation of their places the great object of their adminiſtration. Yes, ye tame and ſordid [illegible], you have betrayed the nation to the enemy, in order to ſecure the loaves and fiſhes. You knew that war would prove fatal to you, as miniſters, that you could not a moment longer exiſt as the rulers of this once mighty nation. You [illegible] your plan of domeſtic poli- [illegible] he affections of the King's ſubjects, and that, as I ſaid once before, he would go to war with only half his people at his back. Yet rather than let go your hold of the mammon of unrighteouſneſs, you ſacrificed your king and your country.

Indeed the ſafety of your heads required this error. For had you deſcended from the high ſtation which you now hold, I ſuſpect you would have only deſcended in order to aſcend to a ſtill higher poſt. Now you think yourſelves ſecure. But believe me, you are, like felons, reprieved only for a month or two. *Impii tolluntur in altum ut caſu graviore ruant.* You are only filling up the meaſure of your iniquity. The cup will ſoon run over. A day of reckoning will come, and I hope it will come, not in a time of coolneſs, but in a time of warmth, when the people, enraged with your violence at home, and treachery abroad, will demand ſignal vengeance on thoſe who dared to patch up this ignominious convention, this temporary and ſhort lived truce, which gives ſo deep a wound, ſo fatal a ſtab, to the honour of England. Yes, ſir, we are ſtabbed to the heart. I feel it, you muſt feel it, all England will feel and rue it. Shall it not then be required at their hands? Yes, blood will have blood, and I hope England will, as an atonement, ſhed the blood of the traitors. If this act of juſtice does not take place, if an example is not made of bad miniſters, we are a ruined and undone nation. They will go on fearleſsly in the ſame career, till our power, and wealth, and liberty, crumble to pieces, and melt away like the baſeleſs fabrick of a viſion, and leave but a wreck behind.

Why, the very friends and props of adminiſtration condemn this tranſaction in private. And ſhall they come here to vote that right, which in their conſciences they think wrong? Is this the only place in which Engliſhmen dare not ſpeak their genuine ſentiments

sentiments ?----No wonder that this house has lost its authority, when its resolutions are determined by such slaves and such misers? When I advised the minister to insist on indemnification, and a reimbursement of the expence, he answered, what, all the expence! Sure you cannot expect all! But behold! instead of securing all, he has not secured any part, no, not a single farthing. Yet where is the wonder, when he could accept, as an adequate satisfaction, a declaration, that contains an absolute, a palpable falshood? The king of Spain considering the reciprocality of amicible and pacific sentiments, with which he and the king of Great-Britain are inspired! Can you help expressing your contempt at such disingenuity on one side, and such simplicity on the other! Why there is not a single minister, nor a single member of this house, that believes Spain to to be inclined to peace ——Every man in England, every man in Europe, knows the reverse. It is notorious that the king of Spain was reluctantly forced to acquiesce in this declaration, humiliating as it is to England, by the distraction of France, and the weakness of the French ministry, whom, tho you had an opportunity of dissolving the Family Compact, you have allowed to dupe you, and to carry off immense sums gained in your stocks. But why do I say *dupe you?* You duped the public. Some of the highest among you joined the foreign harpies, the French and Spanish leeches, who in the alley swill the sweat of the poor, and gorge themselves with the blood of the widow and the orphan. But here let me stop. Not that I have not more to say. When the proper time comes, if I do not let you hear more, you may tell me of it.

———

CHARLES F——X *spoke next.*

SIR,

IF there are speakers, who, without giving light, puzzle with smoke, there are others, who dazzle and confound with fire and flame. If they are neither Torpedoes, nor Scuttle-fishes, nor Smoke-Jacks, they are *Ignes Fatui*, Wills with the Whisp, that bewilder the followers, and betray them at last into worse than Hibernian bogs and quagmires. Which then of the two is the more dangerous, a glimmering taper, or a flaming meteor? The former, however feeble, is still a friendly light; but the latter portends destruction and death. *Prophet of Ills*, a lying spirit has, I hope, gone out of thy mouth; nor will thy hoarse accents be more regarded in this enlightened assembly, than the croakings of a raven are in this learned age. As we can separate truth from falshood, we can distinguish the clamours of faction from the voice of patriotism. Away then with your ominous predictions. They are only the feverish dreams of an overheated imagination, the mere delerium of a man that believes, because he wishes them true. What but the same cause produced the late false and scandalous charges against the judges? When the rage of faction could not spare such venerable men, why should we be surprised at this savage attack? The wonder would be if we escaped that violence and fury which have held nothing sacred, which have impiously aimed at the very throne. But who does not despise your impotent attempts? As well might the wicked band of giants expect to scale heaven, and to snatch the thunder from the hand of Jove. The objects of your envy are far above your reach. In vain you pile hill upon hill, and mountain upon mountain, Ossa upon Pelion, and Pindus on Ossa. They stand secure upon the lofty top of Olympus, and laugh you to scorn. They regard you no more than a parcel of ants building their hill in the valley below.

But the honourable gentleman has charged a [illegible] with having promiſed better, with having aſſured this houſe that Spain ſhould pay a part of our expence. On what does he found his aſſertion? On the faithfulneſs of his own memory! without offering any affront to his memory, or impeaching his veracity, I hope other gentlemen will be allowed to truſt as much to their recollection; and then, if memory contradict memory, his teſtimony will be deſtroyed by contrary teſtimony, and be as if it had never been. Sure I am that my attendance on my duty in this houſe, has been punctual. Few have been ſeldomer abſent. Yet I muſt ſay, that no traces of the alledged expreſſions remain on my memory. Other members give the ſame evidence, and corroborate the preſumptive proof. Though they have not ſpoke, they will declare this circumſtance to any man that conſults them. Shall we then truſt a ſingle memory in preference to ſo many? Or, what is the ſame, ſhall we make the evidence of a ſolitary individual outweigh that of a whole cloud of witneſſes? The idea is too abſurd, too groſs to be ſwallowed. We muſt conclude that it is one of the gentleman's dreams, one morning before he was awake, when his buſy brain was building caſtles, and ſtorming the laſt redoubt of the miniſtry.

As to the objections made to the motion, I think them extremely juſt, and well founded.---The deſign of oppoſition in taking the obnoxious words from the king's ſpeech, and inſerting them in the motion, is evident.——They meant to return them back upon the king and his miniſters, as proofs of non-performance of promiſe, and of inattention to the national intereſt. Here, ſaid they, our rights are declared to have been deeply affected. If we can perſuade the public that they are his majeſty's words, they will naturally aſk,---Why did he not then aſſert theſe rights, and oblige the proud Spaniard to own them in his declaration? In this manner they reaſoned. And now they are ſo obſtinate as to contend that theſe are his majeſty's very words.——They are ſo, but then they are not all his words. The ſpeech ſays, that the *honour of the crown and the ſecurity of our rights were deeply affected*. The motion ſays, that *our rights were deeply affected*. Now there is an evident difference between *our rights* and the *ſecurity of our rights*. Therefore it is in vain that you aſſert the words in both papers to be literally the ſame, while you leave out ſome, and while thoſe that you retain differ eſſentially in their meaning and import. Ceaſe, then, to confound two diſtinct ideas, and to perplex us with your want of preciſion. The objects in queſtion were very judiciouſly kept ſeparate by the miniſter, who juſtly concluded that both were ſupplied for preſerving the honour of the crown.

———

Lord N——h's Reply.

SIR,

IT always gives me pain to conſume the time of this reſpectable aſſembly in the diſcuſſion of light and frivolous queſtions. I have too much veneration for it to be guilty of ſuch a treſpaſs. Were the objection made to the motion of this nature, I would be the firſt to let it drop. But, convinced as I am of the reverſe, I cannot allow complaiſance ſo far to get the better of prudence as to ſuffer the motion to paſs in its preſent form. Not that I mean to retract my former words, and to make an oppoſition to all its contents. No, Sir, I am not ſo fickle. Notwithſtanding the dreadful ſhapes, and monſtrous forms, which have been ſet before my eyes, I am ready, as far as in my lies, to give you all the papers that can convey any information, or, indeed, that exiſt. All the alteration that, after ſecond thoughts, I deſire, is confined to a ſingle word, to the word *were*, and that abſolutely *muſt* be altered. Else now can you pretend, according to the [illegible] deſign of the obnoxi-

ous

ous clause, to echo back his majesty's meaning? Change *were* into *was*, and there will be no room for cavil. At least you will not hear a single word more from me on this head.

I know not whether I shall find it so easy to adjust matters between myself and the gentleman who charges me with a breach of promise. He says I pledged myself to this assembly that no accommodation should take place, except Spain engaged to defray a part of the expence to which we had been put, in consequence of the violence committed by the governor of *Buenos Ayres*. Where could he pick up this anecdote? Surely not from my lips. My words, rightly understood, could never have given birth to this fable. He must certainly have misconceived, or misinterpreted my expressions. The whole current of my conversation, not only in public, but in prevate, has invariably run in a different channel. Nor have I the faintest traces of such language now upon my memory. I am therefore morally certain, that I never uttered a syllable, which, without being violently wrested, could bear this construction.

Colonel B—R— E's *Reply.*

SIR,

I need not be surprised that the noble lord does not remember what he said or meant above a month ago, when he cannot remember what I said and meant a few minutes ago. I never insinuated that he had pledged himself for any thing to this house. No, let me do him justice. He could never be brought to any explicit declaration. Always vague and evasive, he cautiously avoided every expression that could tend to remove our apprehensions, or to give us the least assurance that he would not betray the rights of the nation. No wonder then if he thinks the charge may be safely denied. Ministers and courtiers are allowed to be forgetful of their word. I hope he does not confound the ideas of forgetting and denying, and assume the latter also as a privilege of his station. Certain I am that he would hardly give up the point, when I had taken down his words. How much less needs he do it on this occasion, when I have no such advantage on my side? I hate flat contradiction, both because it has the appearance of rudeness, and because it always leaves behind an imputation on the head or heart of the worsted party. I have already had more altercations with the noble lord than I could have willed, but as I have always endeavoured to make them as polite as the nature of the subject would bear, I cannot think myself in any respect blameable. I am still actuated by the same principles. Yet I must not allow politeness to supercede justice. In vindication of my own character I must aver, that several members of parliament, whom I consulted on this head, declare that they remember the minister's words, such as I have represented them, extremely well. What then becomes of Reynard's contrary testimony, and cloud of witnesses? a thousand negative testimonies are destroyed by one positive testimony. But I understand him. He intends, in imitation of his friend, a certain chief justice, to establish a new rule of evidence.

E— D B— RKE *spoke next.*

SIR,

I entirely agree with those gentlemen, who assert that the honour of the crown, and the rights of the people, cannot be separated in idea, and that he who preserves the former, cannot relinquish the latter. They are certainly right. These two points must always follow one another. In domestic concern, the honour of the crown is only sullied, when the rights of the people are invaded, and in foreign [illegible] it is only sullied, when they

they are betrayed. For what is the honour of the crown but the honour of the people? His majeſty, though not ſtrictly and in word only a repreſentative as this houſe is, ſtill is a repreſentative, eſpecially in matters of war and peace, where he acts for the whole community. I only wiſh that his miniſters had always ſquared their conduct by this rule, by this large and extenſive ſenſe, which they have now given to the honour of the crown. We ſhould not then have reaſon to complain, that they have betrayed our rights, and conſequently that very honour, of which, for reaſons well known to themſelves, they pretend to be ſo tenacious. I ſay, 'conſequently betrayed that very honour.' For, if the preſervation of the crown's honour implies the preſervation of the people's rights, I am ſure that, *à fortiori*, the relinquiſhment of the people's rights implies the relinquiſhment of the crown's honour. The propoſition is evidently convertible. The neceſſary connection ſubſiſting between the ſubject and the predicate, render their places mutually interchangeable. Now that the rights of the people have been betrayed is, I think, obvious to the meaneſt capacity. For where is there any ſatisfaction for the injury received, or any reimburſement of the expence incurred, in conſequence of that injury? Inſtead of compenſation you have a declaration, a promiſe from Spain that ſhe will obſerve that faith which ſhe has ſo lately violated, though in that very promiſe ſhe reſerves the right of reſuming the quarrel. O rare negotiators! O able ſtateſmen!

After this inſtance of their wiſdom, why ſhould we wonder to hear them quibbling about the difference between our rights, and the ſecurity of our rights? Without the rights, what ſignifies the ſecurity? Are we here the ſecurity what ſignify the rights? They are inſeparably connected, and we muſt have both, or none. To what purpoſe, then, is all this diſplay of jeſuitical ſubtilty, and dialectical acumen? However juſt the diſtinction may be in logic, it is in politics totally contemptible. The only thing which it has taught us is, that little objects will always engage little minds, and that the king's ſpeech is equivocal. This equivocation, and thoſe quibbles, may do well enough in the narrow circle of the cabal. They may ſatisfy a junto of the miniſter's friends, or rather humble ſervants. They may think that the conformity between the conduct of the miniſtry, and the meaning aſſigned to his majeſty's ſpeech, is a ſufficient vindication of the convention. But the nation will not be ſo complaiſant. It muſt have ſomething more firm and ſubſtantial than theſe quirks and quiddities, which would have been unworthy even of Gill Blas, when he was a ſtudent at Salamanca, and challenged every paſſenger in the ſtreets to a trial of logical ſkill. Their indignation at this ſhameful treaty will, I doubt not, equal that of the honourable member who has been ſo free with the miniſtry, and given you a ſpecimen of the language, which will ſhortly be held by the whole body of the people. Not that I do not think his harangue premature. Yes, Sir, however juſt and ſuitable to the ſubject his honeſt warmth might be, it was certainly ill timed. The terrors of this houſe, to its honour be it ſpoken, are not for miniſters, but for the people. The contemptuous laugh, which run, like an electrical fire, along thoſe benches, at the very idea of bringing a miniſter to account, proves my aſſertion. Indeed nothing can be more abſurd than ſuch a notion. Well may you, gentlemen, ſmile and ſay in your hearts, what bring to account your lord and maſter! No, no. If the ſhepherd, that feedeth us with his hand, and leadeth us forth to green paſtures, be loſt we the flock will be ſcattered abroad,

abroad, and become the prey of wolves.

I know that you are not fond of much argumentation. Instead of reasoning you would choose to divide. I will not, therefore, enter into a full discussion of this negotiation till the papers called for by the motion appear. You will only allow me to make a few remarks on what appears from the *prima facie* evidence, by which, I am sure, it stands condemned.

* This house is universally contemned, and, by heaven, it is truly contemptible. Now it exhibits the confusion of a Polish diet, without the spirit. There is blood in this affair. -- The subject is important, yet you will not hear. I have not spoke absurdly, why then all this disorder? Are you resolved to violate all decorum, and to become a greater bear garden than the upper h——e? For shame! If you are determined to vote without hearing reason, yet still preserve appearances, preserve the semblance of deliberation and counsel. Sit still, for, if you will not, I am resolved to do my duty. I will lift up my voice in the senate, and, if I can do no more, bear testimony against every pernicious measure, and particularly against this scandalous accommodation, which carries on its face so many marks of incapacity and treachery.

At the beginning of the session, the king's speech informed us, that due care should be taken of our rights, and of our honour. The words seemed to promise some spirit and magnanimity. Trusting to this information and this promise, we concurred with him in every instance, and voted the most liberal grants. We gave rather prematurely five hundred thousand pounds of land-tax, four hundred thousand pounds of East-India stock, and the whole produce of the sinking fund, which surely does not fall short of the three millions sterling. The total undoubtedly exceeds four millions. To these grants we added thirteen thousand land forces, and forty thousand seamen. His majesty then, with four millions in his pocket, with thirteen thousand additional land forces, forty thousand seamen, and forty ships of the line, goes to treat with the Spaniards, and what does he bring us back? Why these two bits of paper! O humiliating! Is this the first act of magnanimity, this the first burst of heroism of a king of Great Britain! Well may this transaction be called a mountain in labour of a mouse. Not that I blame his majesty. No, Sir, he is all good, all gracious, and wise. I only complain of his ministers, of his advisers, who were weak or wicked enough to persuade him not to insist upon a compensation for our expence. For I hold it to be a clear and indisputable truth, that the aggressor is accountable, not only for the original injury, but also for all its consequences. Else how could society subsist? The greatest and the most powerful nation might upon any other plan be ruined by the least and the meanest. This mighty empire might be undone by the most pitiful state in Europe. Nay, a savage American tribe, or a horde of naked East-Indians, might prove our destruction. They would have nothing to do but to commit some act of hostility, which would cost us four or five millions in preparations, then to make a simple restitution of the possessions which they had violently seized, and thus to go on with a succession of injuries and restitutions, till they had exhausted our wealth and strength, and broke our spirit and courage.

[illegible] that [illegible] what now [illegible]

* "Here many members got up in order to go to dinner, and there was so much confusion and noise in the house, that he could not be heard. -- For a minute therefore he sat down.

negotiation from the beginning, the ministers needed not to be afraid of its being disturbed. When we called some time ago for papers, the minister's answer was, oh! by no means, would you disturb the negotiation? Consider the punctilios, the etiquette of courts, and the delicacy of Spanish honour. Your interference may make the bird fly out of the cage, before we can shut the door. We may absolutely lose the eel, which we have by the tail. Well, we kept aloof, and they succeeded. They caught, or rather created this eel. But what sort of a creature is it? Much like its creators. Their skill shines throughout its whole frame. Eight long months has it employed three crowned heads, celebrated for wisdom. Eight long months has it employed three ministries, the English, the French, and Spanish. Eight long months has it been the study of a lord of our treasury, and the work, the manufacture of five secretaries of state, and a lord privy seal. First came lord Weymouth, who will never be so much known by his share in this negotiation, as by his negotiation in St George's Fields. Then came lord Hillsborough, so famous for his skill in American negotiations, then lord Sandwich, so much respected for his negotiations with Kidgel, then lord Halifax so renowned for various negotiations, then lord Rochford, whom God bless for his negotiation; and lastly, the virgin privy seal. In short, all of them are remarkable for some kind of negotiation or other. But what has been the effect of their joint efforts on this occasion? That thing upon your table, which I can compare to nothing but to a Birmingham button, that, after passing through twenty hands, may at last be sold for three farthings a gross. I see nothing to be praised in the convention, but its shortness. Here you have the wisdom of the [illegible] in a nut-shell. As they have [illegible] a barren rock, so they have taken care to render the treaty correspondent. Like its object, it is little, cold, and barren.

From the Manuscript of Sir JAMES WARE.

QUEEN MARY having dealt severely with the protestants in England, about the latter end of her reign, signed a commission for to take the same course with them in Ireland, and to execute the same with greater force, she nominates Dr Cole one of the commissioners. This doctor coming with the commission to Chester, on his journey, the mayor of that city, hearing that her majesty was sending a messenger into Ireland, and he being a churchman, waited on the doctor, who, in discourse with the mayor, taking out of a cloak-bag a leather box, saying unto him, "Here is a commission that shall lash the heretics in Ireland," calling the protestants by that name. The good woman of the house, being well affected to the protestant religion, and having also a brother, named John Edmonds, of the same, then a citizen in Dublin, was much troubled at the doctor's words, but watching her convenient time, while the mayor took his leave, and the doctor complimented him down stairs, she opened the box, takes the commission out, and places in lieu thereof, a sheet of paper, with a pack of cards wrapped up therein, the knave of clubs being placed uppermost. The doctor coming up to his chamber, suspecting nothing of what had been done, put up the box as formerly. The next day, going to the water side, wind and weather serving him, he sails towards Ireland, and landed on the 17th of Oct 1558, at Dublin, then coming to the Castle, the lord Fitz-Walter, being lord-deputy, sent for him to come before him [illegible] council, who coming in, after he had made a speech, relating upon what account he came over, he presents the box unto the lord deputy, who causing it to be opened, that the secretary might read the commission, there was nothing, save a pack of cards, with the knave of clubs uppermost, which not only startled the lord deputy and council, but the doctor, who assured him he had a commission, but knew not how it was gone. Then the lord deputy made answer, "Let us have another commission, and we will shuffle the cards in the mean while." The doctor, being troubled in his mind, went away, and returned into England, and coming to the court, obtained another commission, but staying for a wind on the water side, news came to him that the queen was dead, and thus God preserved the protestants of Ireland.

Queen Elizabeth was so delighted with this story, which was related to her by lord Fitzwalter on his return to England, that she sent for Elizabeth Edmonds, whose husband's name was Mattershead, and gave her a pension of 40l. during her life.—*Harleian Miscellany.*

Memoirs of Sir ANDREW MITCHELL, *of Thainstone, late British Ambassador at the Court of Berlin.*

THIS gentleman was the only child of the Rev. Mr. William Mitchell, one of the ministers of St. Giles, commonly called the high church of Edinburgh. His father was first one of the ministers of Aberdeen, but after his translation in that country, (called his settlement or transportation to Edinburgh) he married a widow lady of 1000l. a year fortune, who had an only child, a daughter, the undoubted heir thereof after her death.

To make sure of the fortune, a match between the two children was concluded, and they were married in 1715, at a time when master Mitchell was but eleven years of age, and young Miss but ten. In the fourth year after their nuptials the lady died in child-bed of her first child, an event which so much affected him that he never married afterward. He discontinued the study of the law, for which his father intended him, applying to amusements, by the advice of friends, in order to conquer that grief, which, as was apprehended, might bring on a lowness of spirits.

This was the original cause of an extensive acquaintance with the principal noblemen and gentlemen in North Britain, which afterwards ensued, and for attaining which he seemed to be naturally formed. Tho' his progress in the sciences was but small, yet no person had a greater regard for learned men. His introduction to the first class was owing to lord president Dalrymple, of the court of session, and that to the second, partly to his being universally known to the clergy, and to the several professors of the university of Edinburgh, which was, at that period, in just repute and esteem.

He was in a particular manner intimately acquainted with Mr. M'Laurin, and though his knowledge of Algebra and mixed quantity was but inconsiderable, yet he employed Mr. Henderson, anno 1736, to write out a copy both of the algebra and treatise of gunnery, which Mr. M'Laurin had wrote with amazing clearness and perspicuity.

By his being known to the Marquis of Tweedale, and the Earl of Stair, he became secretary to the former, on his lordship's being appointed minister of Scots affairs, anno 1741, and in the beginning of 1742, he, on lord Stair's arrival in London, put his lordship in mind of the high regard he had always bore for Dr. Pringle, (now Sir John Pringle) then professor of moral philosophy in the university of Edinburgh. The doctor was at his own houſe in Stone-laws-cloſe, when a letter arrived from Mr Mitchell, dated the 14th of June, 1742, acquainting him that he was appointed phyſician to the Britiſh ambaſſador then at the Hague

Though the marquis of Tweedale reſigned the place of ſecretary of ſtate, in conſequence of the convulſions of the year 1745, yet Mr Mitchell ſtill kept in favour He had taken care, during that memorable winter, to keep up a correſpondence with ſome eminent clergymen, and, from time to time, communicated the intelligence he received, and his aſſiduity was rewarded with a ſeat in the houſe of commons, anno 1747, as repreſentative for the boroughs of Bamff, Elgin, Cullein, Inverary, and Kintore

In the year 1751, he was appointed his majeſty's reſident at Bruſſels, where continuing two years, he, in 1753, came over to London, when he was created a knight of the Bath, and appointed ambaſſador extraordinary and plenipotentiary at the court of Pruſſia, where, by his polite and genteel behaviour, and a previous acquaintance with Marſhal Keith, he gained ſo much upon the perſon of his Pruſſian majeſty as to detach him from the French intereſt, an event which involved the court of France in the greateſt loſſes, ariſing not only from vaſt and uncommon ſubſidies to the courts of Vienna, Peterſburgh, and Stockholm, but from the loſs of more numerous armies than ever they had been ſtripped of ſince the reign of Francis I

He generally accompanied the king through the courſe of his ſeveral campaigns, and on the 12th of Auguſt, 1759, when the Pruſſian army was totally routed by count Soltikoff, the Muſcovite general, he with difficulty could be prevailed upon to quit the king's tent even while all was in confuſion By his prudent management the late Earl Marſhal of Scotland was introduced to the favour of his majeſty king George II anno 1760 In 1765 he again came over to England for the recovery of his health, which was ſomewhat impaired, ſpent ſome time at Tunbridge Wells, (where the author of this narrative ſaw and converſed with him) and March 1766, again returned to Berlin That year he was honoured in a particular manner at the marriage of the Prince of Orange with the Princeſs Royal of Pruſſia, the king always expreſſing the higheſt regard to his perſonal merits and accompliſhments, for though he was a very temperate man, and ſhunned pomp and oſtentation in his own perſon, yet no man had more at heart the ſupporting the dignity of the ſovereign whom he repreſented

In a word, though not a man of great learning, or outward ſhew, yet he was, in complex, the fine gentleman, and poſſeſſed of real goodneſs of heart

The court of Pruſſia honoured his funeral with their preſence, and the king himſelf, from a balcony, beheld the proceſſion with tears.

A CORRECT *Copy of the* LORDS PROTEST, *againſt approving of the late Convention with Spain*

DISSENTIENT

I. BECAUSE it is highly unſuitable to the wiſdom and gravity of this houſe, and to the reſpect which we owe to his majeſty and ourſelves, to carry up to the throne an addreſs, approving the acceptance of an imperfect inſtrument which has neither been previouſly authoriſed by any ſpecial *full powers* produced by the Spaniſh miniſter, nor been as yet ratified by the king of Spain If the ratification on the part of Spain ſhould be refuſed the addreſs of this houſe will appear no better than an act of precipitate adulation to miniſters, which will juſtly expoſe the peerage of the kingdom to the indignation

dignation of their country, and to the deriſion of all Europe

II Becauſe it is a direct inſult on the feelings and underſtanding of the people of Great Britain to approve this declaration and acceptance, as a means of ſecuring our own and the general tranquillity, whilſt the greateſt preparations for war are making both by ſea and land, and whilſt the practice of preſſing is continued, as in times of the moſt urgent neceſſity, to the extreme inconvenience of trade and commerce, and with the greateſt hardſhips to one of the moſt meritorious and uſeful orders of his majeſty's ſubjects

III Becauſe the refuſing to put the queſtions to the judges upon points of law very eſſentially affecting this great queſtion, and the refuſing to addreſs his majeſty to give orders for laying before this houſe the inſtructions relating to Falkland's Iſlands, given to the commanders of his majeſty's ſhips employed there, is depriving us of ſuch lights as ſeemed highly proper for us on this occaſion

IV Becauſe, from the declaration and correſpondence laid before us, we are of opinion that the miniſters merit the cenſure of this houſe, rather than any degree of commendation, on account of ſeveral improper acts, and equally improper omiſſions, from the beginning to the cloſe of this tranſaction

For it is aſſerted by the Spaniſh miniſter, and ſtands uncontradicted by ours, that ſeveral diſcuſſions had paſſed between the miniſters of the two courts, upon the ſubject of Falkland's Iſland, which might give the Britiſh miniſters reaſon to foreſee the attack upon that ſettlement that was afterwards made by the forces of Spain Capt Hunt alſo arriving from thence ſo early as the third of June laſt, did advertiſe the miniſters of repeated warnings and menaces made by Spaniſh governors and commanders of ſhips of war, yet ſo obſtinately negligent and ſupine were his majeſty's miniſters, and ſo far from the vigilance and activity required by the truſt and duty of their offices, that they did not even ſo much as make a ſingle repreſentation to the court of Madrid, which, if they had done, the injury itſelf might have been prevented, or at leaſt ſo ſpeedily repaired, as to render unneceſſary the enormous expences to which this nation has been compelled, by waiting until the blow had been actually ſtruck, and the news of ſo ſignal an inſult to the crown of Great Britain had arrived in Europe To this wilful, and therefore culpable, neglect of repreſentation to the court of Spain, was added another neglect; a neglect of ſuch timely preparation for putting this nation in ſuch a ſtate of defence, as the menacing appearances on the part of Spain, and the critical condition of Europe required. Theſe preparations, had they been undertaken early, would have been executed with more effect, and leſs expence, would have been far leſs diſtreſſing to our trade, and to our ſeamen, would have authoriſed us in the beginning to have demanded, and would in all probability have induced Spain to conſent to, an immediate, perfect, and equitable ſettlement of all the points in diſcuſſion between the two crowns, but all preparation having been neglected, the national ſafety was left depending rather upon accidental alterations in the internal circumſtances of our neighbours, than in the proper and natural ſtrength of the kingdom, and this negligence was highly aggravated by the refuſal of adminiſtration to conſent to an addreſs propoſed by a noble lord, in this houſe, laſt ſeſſions, for a moderate and gradual augmentation of our naval forces

V Becauſe the negotiation, entered into much too late, was, from the commencement, conducted upon principles as diſadvantageous to the wiſdom of our public councils, as it was finally concluded in a manner disgraceful to the honour of the crown of Great Britain, for it appears, that the court of Madrid did disavow the act of hostility, as proceeding from *particular* instructions, but justified it under her *general* instructions to her governors, under the oath by them taken, and under the established laws of America This general order was never disavowed nor explained, nor was any disavowal or explanation thereof ever demanded by our ministers, and we apprehend that this justification of an act of violence under *general orders*, *established laws*, and *oaths of office*, to be far more dangerous and injurious to this kingdom, than the particular enterprize which has been disavowed, as it evidently supposes, that the governors of the Spanish American provinces, are not only authorised, but required without any particular instructions, to raise great forces by sea and land, and to invade his majesty's possessions in that part of the world, in the midst of profound peace

VI Because this power, so unprecedented and alarming, under which the Spanish governor was justified by his court, rendered it the duty of our ministers to insist upon some censure or punishment, upon that governor, in order to demonstrate the sincerity of the court of Madrid, and of her desire to preserve peace, by putting at least some check upon those exorbitant powers asserted by the court of Spain to be given to her governors But although our ministers were authorised not only by the acknowledged principles of the law of nations to call for such censure or punishment, but also by the express provision of the [illegible]enteenth article of the treaty of Utrecht, yet they have thought fit to observe a profound silence on this necessary article of public reparation If it were thought that any [illegible] appeared in the [illegible] or pardon of the punishment adviseable, that abatement or pardon ought to have been the effect of his majesty's clemency, and not an impunity to him, arising from the ignorance of our ministers in the first principles of public law or their negligence or pusillanimity in asserting them

VII Because nothing has been had or demanded as a reparation in damage for the enormous expence and other inconveniencies arising from the confessed and unprovoked violence of the Spanish forces in the enterprize against Falkland's islands, and the long subsequent delay of justice, it was not necessary to this demand that it should be made in any improper or offensive language, but in that stile of accommodation which has ever been used by able negotiators

VIII Because an unparalleled and most audacious insult has been offered to the honour of the British flag, by the detention of a ship of war of his majesty's, for twenty days after the surrender of Port Egmont, and by the indignity of forcibly taking away her rudder, this act could not be supported upon any idea of being necessary to the reduction of the fort, nor was any such necessity pretended No reparation in honour has been demanded for this wanton insult, by which his majesty's reign is rendered the unhappy æra in which the honour of the British flag has suffered the first stain with entire impunity

IX Because the Spanish declaration, which our ministers have advised his majesty to accept, does in general words imply his majesty's disavowal of some acts on his part tending to disturb the good correspondence of the two courts, when it is notorious, that no act of violence whatsoever had been committed on the part of Great Britain by this disavowal of some implied aggression in the very declaration, pretended to be made for reparation of the injured dignity of Great Britain, his

ma[illegible]

majeſty is made to admit a ſuppoſition contrary to the truth, and injurious to the dignity and honour of the crown.

X Becauſe in the ſaid declaration, the reſtitution is confined to port Egmont, when Spain herſelf originally offered to cede Falkland's Iſlands, it is known that ſhe made her forcible attack on pretence of title to the whole, and the reſtitution ought, therefore, not to have been confined to a part only, nor can any reaſon be aſſigned, why the reſtitution ought to have been made in narrower or more ambiguous words than the claims of Spain, on which her act of violence was grounded, and her offers of reſtitution originally made

XI Becauſe the declaration, by which his majeſty is to obtain poſſeſſion of port Egmont, contains a reſervation or condition of the queſtion of a claim of prior right of ſovereignty in the catholic king to the whole of Falkland's Iſlands, being the firſt time ſuch a claim has ever authentically appeared in any public inſtrument, jointly concluded on by the two courts No explanation of the principles of this claim has been required, although there is juſt reaſon to believe that theſe principles will equally extend to reſtrain the liberty, and confine the extent of the Britiſh navigation No counter claim has been made on the part of his majeſty to the right of ſovereignty, in any part of the ſaid iſland ceded to him, any aſſertion whatſoever of his majeſty's right of ſovereignty, has been ſtudiouſly avoided, from the beginning to the accompliſhment of this unhappy tranſaction, which, after the expence of millions, ſettles no conteſt, aſſerts no right, exacts no reparation, affords no ſecurity, but ſtands as a monument of reproach to the wiſdom of the national councils, of diſhonour to the eſſential dignity of his majeſty's crown, and of diſgrace to the hitherto untainted honour of the Britiſh flag

After having given theſe reaſons, founded on the facts which appeared from the papers, we think it neceſſary here to diſclaim an invidious and injurious imputation, ſubſtituted in the place of fair argument, that they who will not approve of this convention, are for precipitating their country into the calamities of war we are as far from the deſign, and we truſt much farther from the act of kindling the flame of war, than thoſe who have adviſed his majeſty to accept of the declaration of the Spaniſh ambaſſador

We have never entertained the leaſt thought of invalidating this public act, but if miniſters may not be cenſured, or even puniſhed for treaties which, though valid, are injurious to the national intereſt and honour, without a ſuppoſition of the breach of public faith in this houſe, that ſhould cenſure or puniſh, or of a breach of the laws of humanity in thoſe who propoſe ſuch cenſure or puniſhment, the uſe of the peers as a controul on miniſters, and the beſt as well as higheſt, council of the crown, will be rendered of no avail We have no doubt but a declaration more adequate to our juſt pretenſions, and to the dignity of the crown, might have been obtained without effuſion of blood, not only from the favourable circumſtances of the conjuncture, but becauſe our juſt demands were no more than any ſovereign power, who had injured another thro' inadvertence or raſhneſs, ought, even from regard to its own honour, to have granted and we are ſatiſfied, that the obtaining ſuch terms would have been the only means of eſtabliſhing a laſting and honourable peace

Richmond, [illegible]
Bolton, King,
Mancheſter, Torrington,
Tankerville, Vernon,
[illegible] [illegible]
Wycombe [illegible]
[illegible] [illegible]
[illegible]

[illegible], Scarborough,
Ponsonby, Archer

Dissentient,

Because, though the disavowal may be considered as humiliating to the court of Spain, the declaration and acceptance, under the reservation of the question of prior right, do not, in my opinion, after the heavy expences incurred either convey a satisfaction adequate to the insult on the honour of Great Britain, or afford any reasonable grounds to believe that peace, on terms of honour can be lasting.

RADNOR.

The Helmet. An Anecdote.

THAT brave captain Lopez D'Acunha, arming himself in haste for a sudden enterprize, cries to one of his attendants who was equipping him, "Pray fix on my helmet better, it hurts my ear intolerably." His attendant insisted it could not be better fixed; he, without disputing the matter further, sets off to where danger and glory called. At his return, with the greatest composure, he throws his helmet on the ground with his ear in it, and with the most calm aspect, turns to his servant, "there," says he pointing to it, "did I not tell you it was badly fixed."

On Gaming.

IB[illegible] ed, [illegible] [illegible] misery [illegible] a corner with [illegible] wretched [illegible] [illegible]

but, it were much to be wished, that some more certain means could be found to alleviate this distress, not by laying taxes on the industrious, but on luxury, and making private vices subservient to the public good.

Gaming seems to be the prevailing vice of the age, which has so infected every stage of life in both sexes, more particularly the female, that the rational amusements of music or the theatre, are now totally exploded. Handel and Shakespear are as much forgotten, as if they never had existed, and, in their places, we hear of routs and parties carried on for the purposes of scandal and gaming. I fear admonition or satyr would be equally vain. Come then, Mr printer, with your rod of scorpions, or if corporal punishment should be thought too severe, let a poll tax be levied on all ladies, who have arrived at a certain age, grown callous to all the feelings of humanity, and forgetting what they owe their families and themselves, devote their whole time to the card-table; there the silent spectator may see this vice in all its deformity; the grave matron acting the sharper, raising one minute [illegible] fortune, and the next at her partner. Perhaps, it might not be entirely useless to present to the public the outlines of some characters, who [illegible] sure trade of cards, [illegible] of Seneca or the Whole Duty of Man, has initiated [illegible] into the mysteries of all the present fashionable games, prudently foreseeing, that neither their [illegible] required accomplishments were likely to advance their fortunes. This grave lady [illegible] to a party with more eagerness [illegible] the hungry labourer to his [illegible], and seizes the cards as a tyger [illegible] his prey, being sure to [illegible] the unhappy victims of her [illegible] woman should be esteemed reprobate and irreclaimable, [illegible] therefore be [illegible] by the

the grand jury, as the bane of society and a public nuisance.

If you think the above worthy of being inserted, I shall, in my next, present you with some more of this creditable groupe.

ACADEMICUS.

Theatrical Chronicle.

Crow-Street Theatre, Nov 9, 1771.

IT is really astonishing to any person, who has seen this place, when Stretch's puppet show, to think it possible so wretched a hovel could be converted into so neat a little theatre; but we must lament that the manager, who certainly have done every thing to give us the best entertainment we have had for some years, should, by the smallness of the house, which we are informed cannot contain more than about 70 l. be excluded from reaping the benefit they are so justly intitled to, they opened their house this night with

The Beggar's Opera, and the Apprentice.

Nov. 13. The Suspicious Husband.

The public has a deserved partiality for Mr Lewis, particularly in his playing Ranger. This young gentleman is decent in every character, and in his line of acting may justly be called a good second rate player.

Nov. 17. Love in a Village, with the Anatomist.

Mr Chapman, who, it is said, never appeared on any stage, performed the part of young Meadows; his voice is true but not sweet; we cannot say his person or performance gave much pleasure; however, he may have mistaken his talent, and give greater satisfaction in another cast of playing.

It were much to be wished miss Ashmore had more spirit in the part of Rosetta, and not attempt, by way of supplying this defect, to imitate the witless buffoonery of miss Catley, whose follies are overlooked in consideration of her agreeable person and inchanting voice.

Any person who has not seen Mr Brown's excellence in the character of La Medicine in the Anatomist, must be pleased with Mr. Dodd.

Nov. 19. Love in a Village, with Miss in her Teens.

There is not a player on our stage more improved than Mrs Price, who did miss Biddy Bellair; she gave general satisfaction, and if she took some pains to divest herself of our provincial accent, she would be a useful acquisition to the stage.

Mr Ryder's performance of Fribble has not been excelled.

Nov. 21. Jane Shore, with the Lying Valet.

Miss Young from Drury-lane made her first appearance this night in Jane Shore. To describe every particular of her excellent performance of this character, is out of our power; we shall therefore only make a few remarks on those parts where it would not be doing her justice to be silent.

In her two first speeches in the second scene, with a most elegant and just action, she exhibited all the majesty of grief, but when Dumont tells me was born at Antwerp, remorse, curiosity, and shame could not be better expressed.

> Alas! at Antwerp!—oh forgive my tears!
> They fall for my offences—and must fall
> Long, long e'er they shall wash my stains away.
> You knew perhaps—oh grief, oh shame! my husband.

When Lord Hastings in the 2d act lays hold of her, and unwilling to stand longer parly, says,

> ———Come, let me press thee,
> Pant on [illegible] thy arms,
> And [illegible] the luxurious fold!

anger

anger and ſteady reſolve were viſible in her look, and the raiſing of her voice had an admirable effect in theſe words,

> Never! by thoſe chaſte lights above, I ſwear,
> My ſoul ſhall never know pollution more!
> Forbear, my lord ——

From the terror that ſeizes her when Dumont and Haſtings fight, ſhe gradually ſubſides into a ſettled melancholy,

> O that my head were laid, &c

In the fourth act where Gloſter acquaints her that Haſtings defends the cauſe of Edward's children, our heroine, forgetting her perſonal reſentment againſt Haſtings, ſays,

> Reward him for the noble deed, juſt heaven!
> For this one action, &c. &c

Her expreſſion was here inimitable, her perſon, look, attitude, and voice, were the ſtrongeſt picture of gratitude and joy

In the laſt ſcene her judgment and ſenſibility were no where more apparent, it was impoſſible to behold her without emotion

On the whole, if judgment, ſenſibility, expreſſion, and voice, have any claim to merit, this young gentlewoman bids fair to gain the ſummit of dramatic excellence

Nov. 22 The Suſpicious Huſband, and the Padlock

The town has been always pleaſed with miſs Aſhmore in the Padlock, ſhe has merit in thoſe characters, and we think it is her line of acting

Nov. [illegible] Jane Shore, and the Anatomiſt

Nov. 24 The Buſy Body, with the Devil to pay

Nov. 26 Merchant of Venice, with the Lying Valet

The part of Shylock was performed by Mr Charles Macklin to a crowded audience The managers of this houſe (who are meſſrs Marton, Dawſon, and the widow Hoſkin) have engaged him to perform this ſeaſon on condition of paying him twenty guineas each night of his performance, nor do we think them loſers by the agreement, in the event, having brought them ſuch audiences in the ſubſequent nights of his performance, that there has been an overflow each time

This gentleman's merit as a comedian, in various characters, has been ſo long eſtabliſhed, and is ſo generally known as to need but little comment his particular excellence in the characters of

"Sir Gilbert Wrangle in the Refuſal, Don Manuel in the Kind Impoſtor, Sir Archibald Mac Sarcaſm, Sir Pertinax Mac Sycophant and Murogh o Doherty in his own pieces, would be ſufficient to place him in the firſt rank of comedians, but the part in which as yet he is unequalled is that of "Shylock in the Merchant of Venice," which he performed in ſo natural a manner on his firſt appearance in it, that a gentleman, one of the audience, by way of diſtinction of his ſuperior abilities, ſtarted out into this accidental *extempore*,

> This is the Jew
> That Shakeſpear drew,

which expreſſion, being ready to every one's remembrance, hath eſtabliſhed his very deſerved reputation in that character His merit alſo as an author may be judged by his compoſitions as follows

"Henry the 7th, a tragedy
"True born Scotchman, a comedy
"The married Libertine, a comedy
"The true born Iriſhman, a farce
"Love a la-mode, a farce
"The Fortune Hunter, a farce
"The Suſpicious Huſband criticiſed, a farce
"[illegible] or no Wall, a farce"

But

But to return to his manner of playing Shylock, how great is his expression of distrust in act 1, scene 3

Shy But ships are but boards, sailors but men there be land rats, &c

In the same scene where, after reproaching Antonio, he affects an obsequious smile, and jeeringly proceeds

——Fair Sir, you spit on me last Wednesday,
You spurn'd me such a day, another time
You call'd me dog, and for these curtesies
I'll lend you thus much monies?

And when Antonio, piqued at this, replies,

Ant I am as like to call thee so again, &c

His look is the very picture and voice, the very accent of dissimulation

Shy —Why, how you storm?
I would be friends with you, and have your love,
Forget the shames that you have stain'd me with
Supply your present wants and take no doit
Of usance for my monies, and you'll not hear me
This is kind I offer

In the third act, where, after lamenting to Tubal the loss of his daughter and money, he continues

Shy —— and no satisfaction, no revenge, no ill luck stirring, but what lights o' my shoulders, no sighs but o' my breathing, no tears but o' my shedding

Tubal Yes, other men have ill-luck too, Antonio, as I heard, in Genoa—

Shy What, what what? ill-luck, ill luck

Tubal Hath an Argosie cast away, coming from Tripolis

Shy I thank God, I thank God is it true? is it true

His admirable expression of an hellish joy is beyond description, but his amazing flexibility of tone and muscles is no where more evident than in this transition, where Tubal tells him,

Tub Your daughter spent in Genoa, as I heard, one night fourscore ducats

Shy Thou stick'st a dagger in me I shall never see my gold again—fourscore ducats at a sitting, fourscore ducats!

In the fourth act can there be a stronger character exhibited of inexorable revenge and villany, when he is offered double the principal of the bond?

Shy If every ducat, in six thousand ducats,
Were in six parts, and every part a ducat
I would not draw them, I would have my bond

Nov 27 Beggar's Opera, with miss in her Teens

Nov 29 Provoked Husband, with the Apprentice

Nov 30 By Command of his Excellency the Lord Lieutenant, The Suspicious Husband, and the Lying Valet Boxes free to the ladies.

In our next we shall give an account of the performance at the theatre in Smock-alley

---

An Account of the new Tragedy called Clementina, *as it was acted, for the first time, at the Theatre-Royal in Covent Garden.*

PERSONS *of the* DRAMA

Anselmo	Mr *Savigny*.
Granville	Mr. *Bensley*.
Palermo	Mr *Wroughtor*.
A noble Venetian	Mr *Gardner*
Clementina	Mrs *Yates*
Eliza	Miss *Pearce*

SCENE *lies in* VENICE

Senators, Officers, Guards, Attendants, &c

TIME *About the same with that of the Representation*

THE Republic of Venice, having greatly suffered, not only in consequence of intestine broils, but of her long continued wars with some of the most formidable neighbouring powers, began to receive new vigour from the spirited conduct of one of her senators, named Anselmo who, animated with a patriotic zeal, for the honour and interest of his country, took every method in his power to re-establish her ancient consequence and splendor

Clementina.

Clementina, the only daughter of this nobleman, had unknown to her father, contracted a tender friendship with Rinaldo, a young officer in the service of the state, whose ancestors had made violent opposition to the measures of Anselmo, and were considered as the greatest enemies of his house. A private marriage soon after took place, and made the lovers mutually happy in each other; but Rinaldo being obliged to attend his duty in the field against the foes of his country, after being covered with wounds, was seen to sink amidst a party of his opponents, and an account of his death was immediately carried to Venice.

Overwhelmed with grief at this intelligence, Clementina determined never to enter into a second alliance, and used all endeavours to dissuade her father from encouraging Palermo, a youth of noble birth and great abilities, to pay his addresses to her.

About this juncture the tragedy commences. Clementina, after expressing to her confidant the distracted state of her mind, from the irreparable loss of her beloved Rinaldo, and the continued distressing applications of Anselmo in favour of Palermo, receives a visit from her father, who tenderly reproaches her the want of obedience, and the necessity of her looking on Palermo as her intended husband, in so pathetic a manner, that, penetrated with a sense of filial affection, Clementina faintly consents to listen to the suit of that young nobleman, who is soon after, to his great satisfaction, made acquainted with the successful issue of Anselmo's interview, and, supposing his marriage with Clementina on the point of being celebrated, expresses his gratitude to the venerable senator in the strongest terms.

During these transactions, Rinaldo, who had been left for dead on the field of battle, being perceived to have some signs of life, was taken care of, and recovered by his generous enemies, who, astonished at his valiant exploits, represented them in so striking a manner, that he received uncommon offers of preferment, on condition he entered into the service of the French monarch. As he had little expectation from the power of his opponents, and the decline of his family, of raising himself in the Venetian army, and as he despaired of obtaining Anselmo's approbation of his match with Clementina, in his present condition he resolved to accept the offers that were made him, and advance his fortune in a foreign land. He accordingly changed his name to Granville, and in a short time gave such signal proofs of his talents, that he was loaded with fame and honours. The distracted state of Venice having made it imagined the republic must fall an easy prey to her enemies, the French monarch sent Granville as ambassador to that city, with propositions of friendship, alliance, and protection, provided the Senators would in some slight degree acknowledge him as their sovereign.

This embassy was extremely acceptable to Granville, as he hoped to find some means of seeing his long lost Clementina, (whom he had never been able to inform of his condition) and persuading her to accompany him to France.

On his arrival at Venice he discovered himself to [illegible], who, at the instant Clementina's mind was agitated in the highest degree, from the importunities of Palermo, and when she had determined to die by her own hand, rather than submit to become his wife, acquaints her with the happy news: and an interview, of the most tender nature, soon after takes place between Granville and his amiable spouse, who is extremely solicitous to have him conceal his real name and character, as a law had long subsisted in Venice, perpetually, that

that if any native of that city made the leaſt attempt to alter its conſtitution, he ſhould be puniſhed with death, and as the embaſſy Granville had undertaken made him, if known, amenable to that law. Anſelmo, as head of the ſenate, after a ſhort time gives audience to the ambaſſador from France, and after hearing his propoſals, treats them with the utmoſt indignation.

A writing which Granville produces from his king, veſting the Viceroyſhip of Venice in Anſelmo and his deſcendants, is torn in pieces, in the moſt contemptuous manner, by that honeſt ſenator, who, like a true citizen of a republic, aſſerts the independence of his ſpirit with the utmoſt freedom, and ſhews himſelf an incorruptible and diſintereſted friend to the liberties of his country. After this laudable exertion of his zeal, he tells Granville, notwithſtanding his injurious offer, he ſhall be glad to receive him as a private gentleman, during his reſidence in that city; and retires, in order to prepare for his daughter's marriage with Palermo, who, a ſhort time after, appears in great confuſion, and declares to Anſelmo, that he has diſcovered an intimacy between his daughter and Granville, which gives him the deepeſt concern, and directly mentions having ſeen them together in one of the private receſſes of the garden. Anxious for the honour of his child, Anſelmo flies to the place, and perceives Granville at the inſtant he has embraced her, in conſequence of her having conſented to accompany him in his return to France. Anſelmo, on this detection, loads them with reproaches, commands Granville to be ſeized, and forced on board his veſſel, which, by an order from the ſenate, is obliged to leave the harbour without delay; and, ſuppoſing his darling daughter diſhonoured by a ſtranger, retires in a paroxyſm of grief and deſpair.

This ſcene of domeſtic diſtreſs is followed by one of public reward. The gratitude of Anſelmo's countrymen, for the ſervices he had done the ſtate, aroſe to ſuch a pitch, that they, in open ſenate, invite him to accept of the ſovereign authority, but, with an almoſt unexampled magnanimity, he refuſes the tempting offer, and aſſures them his higheſt ambition is to procure the eſtabliſhment of liberty in the republic, and to free it from the dominion of foreign and domeſtic tyrants, and that he will never accept of any diſtinguiſhed pre-eminence above the reſt of his fellow-citizens. This diſintereſted declaration is received with the loudeſt acclamations by the populace, who conduct him to his houſe in triumph.

Granville, anxious to deliver Clementina from the diſtreſs it muſt naturally be ſuppoſed ſhe was in, after leaving the harbour, determined to make a deſperate effort to carry her off, and accordingly tacked about, and landed a part of his men near Anſelmo's garden, where he preſently obtains the object of his wiſhes; but juſt as they are preparing to embark, Palermo interpoſes, and attacks Granville with great fury, but being overpowered with numbers, he is at length diſarmed, and kept priſoner by Granville's aſſiſtants, who, from the alarm being given, are not able to gain the ſea-beach, but are defeated by the Venetians, who retake Clementina and Palermo, and ſeize Granville, who is immediately thrown into cloſe confinement for his ſuppoſed atrocious behaviour.

Clementina's perturbation of mind, leſt her huſband's real character ſhould be found out, is inexpreſſible, and her father's ill opinion of her, ſhe is hardly able to ſupport. A candid confeſſion of her real ſituation ſeems to her the moſt likely method of terminating her misfortunes; relying, therefore, on the goodneſs of the worthy old nobleman's diſpoſition,

E ſhe

she throws herself at his feet, and declares every transaction that had happened from her first acquaintance with Rinaldo. Affected at the particulars of her story, and happy to find her honour is yet untainted, the good Anselmo congratulates his daughter and himself upon there yet remaining a prospect of happiness, as he doubts not from his great influence to reconcile his son in law with the senate; but the unfortunate Rinaldo having escaped from his confinement, and meeting with his rival Palermo, an honourable termination of their dispute, by single combat, is the consequence of their rencounter, and Rinaldo being mortally wounded, has only strength enough left to present himself before his beloved Clementina, and breathe his last on her bosom. The unhappy lady appears, for some time, torpid with despair; but her passions at length breaking forth, she execrates the authors of her misfortune, and terminates the melancholy story by stabbing herself in a fit of distraction.

The above is a slight sketch (taken from the first representation only) of this interesting tragedy, which abounds with sentiment and theatrical business, and was received with universal applause by the audience. The performers, notwithstanding it is said they got ready in their characters at a very short notice, acquitted themselves with great propriety in their different departments. Not to mention Mrs Yates in particular on this occasion, would be a very unjustifiable omission, as she, through the whole part of Clementina, gave such exquisite proofs of her astonishing theatrical talents, that she frequently produced the most uncommon bursts of approbation from the admiring spectators. The Prologue was spoken by Mr Bensley, and the Epilogue, containing a humourous description of Venice, by Mrs Yates, both which will be laid before the public in a future Magazine.

Observations on modern Education.

Non cuivis Dædaleam *licet omnibus ire* Corinthum.

FRESNOY.

It happens not to every one to see Corinth.

SIR,

YOU have heard it as a common saying, that interest governs the world; but whoever narrowly examines into the particulars, will find that passion, humour, faction, fashion, mode and custom, have as considerable a share in the disposal of human affairs.

I was led into a comment on these matters in my own room last night, after returning from spending the day with a country acquaintance, who treated me with every honest home-spun civility, and loaded my plate with solid pounds of flesh, as a mark of her hospitality. Dinner being over, and every thing settled, the hearth brushed up, the coals thrown on the fire, and the king and queen drank, I began to feel myself rather snug --when on a sudden four children bounced into the room all over treacle, &c -- They were fine babies to be sure. --I patted the head of a boy, and kissed the cheek of a girl, and thought every thing was finished for masters and misses to retire; but alas! I was mistaken. The daughters cried for fruit, and the boys for wine. They were indulged, and while they were playing about upon the carpet, and fighting with each other, the mother pestered me to death with their qualities, and every thing they had said from their earliest infancy. This I bore with philosophy, till she touched upon master Neddy's taste for drawing--- when the father, as if waked from a trance, sprung to his bureau, and spread the table with execrable reams of his son's performances, animadverting, as he went on, upon every

stroke,

ſtroke, tho' as coarſe as if made by a trowel. Not ſatisfied, as I was, with theſe horrid Anti-Raphaelian cartoons, he runs to the nurſery and garret, and brings down an arm full of drawings, without an upright line, in black frames, that he had preſerved as the beſt compoſitions.

At this inſtant a ſervant relieved me with the following letter.

SIR,

YOU have taken ſome unwarrantable liberties with my character, and the firſt time I meet you, you may be certain that I ſhall lay my cane over your ſhoulders, and am,

SIR,

Your humble ſervant.

Tho' this was cavalier, yet it was better than theſe parental hiſtories, which I could not avoid as the menace of my *humble ſervant*.

I have often ſmiled at this concluſion of a letter, which cuſtom and time have given an invariable ſanction to. For what can be more truly ridiculous, than, that after a man has been venting on a ſheet of paper every crudity imaginable, he ſhould politely conclude with aſſuring you that he is

Your very humble ſervant?

The Lawyer declares he will immediately arreſt you, as executor to Mr Lap---if you don't immediately pay him, and is, Sir,

Your very humble ſervant.

The Captain, full of ire, choler, froth and fury, dares you, ſword and piſtol, to the Ring in Hyde-Park, determined to blow out your brains if you meet him; vowing, if you don't come, he will poſt you for a ſcoundrel, and is, Sir,

Your very humble ſervant.

The Huſband, whom you have unluckily cuckolded, finds out his diſhonour, turns the detected lady out of his houſe, ſwears a proſecution againſt you, calls you every name but gentleman, and is, Sir,

Your very humble ſervant.

The Merchant expoſtulates, that you have cozened him in a purchaſe, that you have hurt him by a proteſt of a conſiderable bill, and that you have injured his reputation - but is, Sir,

Your very humble ſervant.

The Honourable Commiſſioners of his Majeſty's Navy tell you, for ſome neglect in your accounts, that they have ſtopped 500l out of your pay, and that they are

Your moſt affectionate friends,
And very humble ſervants.

The Secretaries of the war and navy offices threaten you with the indignation of their different boards - declaring, that in all ſuch caſes you ſhall anſwer it at your peril, and are, Sir,

Your very humble ſervant.

A Criminal, under ſentence, ſolicits for pardon and reſpite, but is told he muſt certainly be hanged, by ſome eaſy gentleman who is

His very humble ſervant.

The Ladies again correſpond in ſimilar forms - and Miſs Biddy, after violently attacking Clara for a ſeduction of her favourite ſwain, tho abſolutely on the margin of matrimony, aſſures her, that ſhe is

Her very humble ſervant.

The penitent Wife, who has only modiſhly cornuted her ſpouſe, tells him, Indeed, my dear, I own I have diſhonoured your bed and my family, and am injured Sir

Your very humble ſervant.

The Virago, who has drove poor Mr Jeremiah Sneak from under his own roof, threatens him vengeance, by the penny-poſt, if he does not return---but is

His affectionate virtuous *wife,*
And very humble ſervant.

It has often amazed me, that cuſtoms of this kind, long eſtabliſhed by time, have not been altered, for ſurely it is a prepoſterous concluſion of an epiſtle, to aſſure a man, whom you have every contempt for, that you are his very humble and obedient ſervant.

I find

I find more or less the manners of people corrected and refined as they approach to the different metropolises. For example, the people of Greenock, Aberdeen, and Perth, are not so polished as those of Edinburgh and Glasgow, nor the inhabitants of Liverpool, Hull, Newcastle, and Plymouth, as those of London. Manners which shock our feelings in town, are not observed in the country, and though many may argue, that though the scabbard is rough on the outside, the sword is bright and sharp within, nevertheless, it is necessary to have even external appearances to recommend us, as well as internal virtues. It has not happened to every person to see London, therefore so much is not expected from the rustic, as the man of education. But I utterly protest against any man professing rudeness, because he can boast of integrity, and is thought to be an honest man. I don't see that the possession of any cardinal virtue entitles any man to be rude and vulgar. Good sense and good manners go hand in hand, and when we lose sight of those two grand leading marks, politeness and civility, be assured the person is at sea, and a dancing master, and good example, are the only pilots that can set him in a right course. The prejudices of parents to their offspring is pardonable, but I have frequently been hurried away from an excellent glass of wine to indulge a fond father, in hearing his daughter squall for an hour to a forte-piano out of tune, without even experience sufficient to strike a right key. I wish some of my friends may read this paper, to save the feelings of the author for the future. Example, in every situation of life, is the best preceptor. But I am sorry to say, that while we have two such exemplary patterns of virtue upon the throne, the nobility of the court are the dupes of gamesters, sharpers, and other infamous adventurers. Were the regal examples such, it would in a small degree plead for the vices of a court, but while such domestic pictures are presented to private life, 'tis pity the subjects have not virtue to imitate their sovereign.

L[illegible] [illegible] d'un Monarque [illegible] et [illegible]
[illegible] [illegible]
[illegible] Auguste [illegible] [illegible] P[illegible]
L[illegible] le Grand Louis [illegible] d'un tendre Amour,
Pa[illegible] de [illegible] Cythere, c'[illegible] la Cour
Quand [illegible] [illegible]
Le [illegible] Cœur [illegible] [illegible]

An Essay on Woman

THOSE who consider women only as pretty figures placed here for ornament, have but a very imperfect idea of the sex. They perpetually say, that women are lovely flowers, designed to heighten the complexion of nature. This is very true, but at the same time women should not let themselves be perverted by such trifling discourse, but take care not to be content with these superficial advantages. There are too many, who, satisfied with that partition, seemed to have renounced any other accomplishment but that of charming the eye. Women have quite another destination, and were created for more noble ends than that of being a vain spectacle, their beauties are only heralds of more touching qualities, to reduce all to beauty is to degrade them, and put them almost on a level with their pictures. Those who are *only* handsome may make a pretty figure in an arm chair, or may decorate a drawing room, they are literally *fit to be seen*, but to find in their acquaintance all the advantages we have a right to expect, women must have more than beauty.

Among intelligent beings, society should not be bounded by a cold exhibition of their persons, or a dull conversation of lies and vanity. Whatever doth not tend to make us better,

better, corrupts us; but if women, who are the ornaments of ſociety, would ſtrive to join juſtneſs of thought and uprightneſs of heart to the graces of the body, the taſte we have for them would unfold excellent qualities in us, let them then raiſe their ſouls to noble objects, and they will ripen the ſeeds of every virtue in men

The empire which women owe to beauty, was only given them for the general good of all the human ſpecies Men, deſtined to great actions, have a certain fierceneſs, which only women can correct; there is in their manners, more than their features, a ſweetneſs, capable of bending that natural ferocity, which untempered would ſoon degenerate into brutality

We may well ſay, that if we were deſtitute of women, we ſhould all be different from what we are Our endeavours to be agreeable to them, poliſh and ſoften that rough ſevere ſtrain ſo natural to us, their chearfulneſs is a counter balance to our rough auſtere humours in a word, if men did not converſe with women, they would be leſs perfect and leſs happy than they are

That man who is inſenſible to the ſweetneſs of female converſation, is rarely the friend to mankind ſuch cheriſh an inſenſibility which render even their virtues dangerous The great qualities of Charles the twelfth, had not troubled all Europe, if that prince had lived more in the ſociety of women, alone capable of ſoftening his untractable courage, for he refuſed to ſee the counteſs of Koninglmarc who brought him, from king Auguſtus, propoſals of peace, which her wit and beauty might have rendered ſucceſsful

If men require the tender application of women to render them more tractable, thoſe on the other hand, equally want the converſation of men to awaken their vivacity, and draw them from a negligence into which [illegible] not ſtimulated by a deſire of pleaſing, they would certainly fall That deſire produces the allurements of the face, the grace of air, and the ſweetneſs of voice. for whether they ſpeak, move, or ſmile, they think of rendering themſelves agreeable Whence we may conclude, that it is the men who, in ſome degree, give charms to the women, who without them would fall into a ſour or indolent temper Beſides, female minds, overwhelmed with trifles would languiſh in ignorance, if men, recalling them to more elevated objects, did not communicate dignity and vigor

'Tis thus that the two ſexes ought to be perfected by one another The manly courage of the one is tempered by the ſoftneſs of the other, which in its turn borrows from the ſame courage The one acquires, in women's company, a milder tincture, while the other loſe their female levity Their different qualities balance each other, and it is from that mixture, that that happy accord ariſes, which renders them both more accompliſhed

The variety of minds may be compared to that of voices, which would rather form an agreeable concert, than a grating diſcord If men are of a ſtronger frame, it is, the more effectually to contribute to the happineſs of thoſe who are more delicate; one ſex was not deſigned to be the oppreſſor of the other the intimate connection between them is for general advantage, and thoſe ridiculous debates of ſuperiority, are an inſult to nature, and an ingratitude for her benefits.

We are born women's friends, not their rivals, much leſs their tyrants and that ſtrength which was given us for their defence, is abuſed when thereby we enſlave them, and to baniſh from ſociety its ſweeteſt charm, that part of the human ſpecies which is moſt proper to animate it, would render it quite inſipid.

The

The truth of this hath been proved by the people of the east, who joining together a sense of their own weakness and a brutal passion, have regarded women as dangerous companions, against whom they must be on their guard: therefore they have enslaved that sex to avoid being enslaved by them, and have thought too much love gave them a title to misuse them. But these tyrannic masters have been the first victims of their tyrannic jealousy. Devoted to a lonely melancholy life, they have sought for tender sensations in vain, amidst their fair slaves. Sensibility, with the delicacy ever its companion, are only to be found in the reign of freedom, since they both necessarily shun a society void of those springs whence they might grow. These and such like people seek to recompense themselves for a lost sensibility and delicacy, by a brutish voluptuousness which only serves to numb their senses, and brutalize their souls.

To the Proprietors *of the* HIBERNIAN MAGAZINE.

Gentlemen,

Your inserting the following Eastern Story in your Monthly Compilation, will, I presume, be acceptable to your readers.

The Supper.

A Certain Sultan of the Indies perceived a woman of exquisite beauty from the roof of his palace; her charms made a strong impression on his mind, and he asked one of his slaves, if he knew who she was? My lord and master, answered the slave, is it possible that your majesty has never heard mention of Chemsennissa * Cadoun, wife to the Vizir Ferouz; she is justly celebrated as the most finished beauty in the city, and her wit is equal to her other charms. These words inflamed the amorous Sultan yet more, and he resolved to find an opportunity of acquainting this miracle of her sex with the sentiments she had inspired. He designed to send the husband out of the way. An Eastern is a very troublesome companion to a person in love with his wife. He sought the Vizir, and giving him a packet, Here, Vizir, said he, execute the order contained in this writing, and render me an account when you have done. Ferouz returned to his house, took up his arms, and went out in such haste, that he forgot the Sultan's order on the [illegible] in his apartment.

Scarce had Ferouz departed, when the impatient Sultan flew with precipitation to the Vizir's palace, and an eunuch introduced him to the chamber of his lady. But judge of her astonishment, at seeing the prince enter! She trembled, and for some time lost the power of utterance; at last, being recovered, she quickly perceived the Sultan's design. But her wit suggested to her, that it was better to prevent an explanation, than run the hazard of disobliging him by a severe reproach; she repeated the following Arabian verses:

'Al meh Sesou [illegible] ugin maik brau
'Miramoun Hauige [illegible] el m[illegible]

The meaning of which [illegible], The lion never dishonours himself by eating the leavings of the wolf, nor will he drink out of the well, whose waters has been sullied by the tongue of the dog *.

The [illegible]

---

* This word signifies in the Arabic tongue, the Sun of Women.

* The Mahometans believe dogs to be impure animals, and never touch them without making an ablution; nevertheless, they breed them like other nations, both for the chase and as guards for the flocks. That species called the dog of the seven sleepers, is much [illegible] among [illegible]

Theſe words, which the Sultan perfectly underſtood, convinced him, that he had nothing to expect, and he retired in ſuch confuſion, as to forget one of his ſlippers, by the lady's bed-ſide.

Meanwhile Feirouz, after ſearching his pockets, recollected that he had left the Sultan's order on the ſofa, in his apartment. He returned to his houſe, the Sultan's ſlipper, which nobody had before perceived, apprized him of the deſign, and of the reaſon for ſending him away. His jealouſy and ambition pointed out the repudiation of his wife, as the only means of preſerving his honour, without incurring the diſpleaſure of his maſter.

He began with giving him an account of his commiſſion, and returning home, acquainted his wife, that the Sultan had preſented him with a very fair palace, and deſired her to paſs ſome days with her father, whilſt he was buſy in providing furniture, he, at the ſame time, gave her an hundred pieces of gold.

Chemſenniſſa, who had nothing wherewith to reproach herſelf, was far from ſuſpecting the truth. She obeyed without reluctance. Many days paſſed, without the appearance of Feirouz, his ſpouſe became alarmed at his indifference, and acquainted her brothers with her fears.

They repaired to the Viſir. 'Explain, ſaid they, 'the motives of your conduct towards your wife: if ſhe be guilty, we are ready to waſh out the ſtain in her blood, but if innocent, why do you diſhonour both us and her, by an unaccountable abſence.'

The viſir not chooſing to unriddle the affair, only anſwered that he had paid her the dower he received from her parents, and that ſhe had no further demand on him. The brothers, provoked by his reply, brought the cauſe before the cadi.

It was the cuſtom of that country, for the Sultan to aſſiſt at all judicial proceedings, that his preſence might retain the magiſtrates within the bounds of their duty.

On coming into the judgment-hall, the brothers * of Chemſenniſſa thus addreſſed the court. 'My Lord, we let this man a delicious garden, filled with every kind of fruit and flower, that could raviſh the eye, or delight the palate. We delivered it to him, in the fineſt ſeaſon, ſurrounded by walls, and fortified with towers. In ſhort, it was an earthly paradiſe. He has plucked the tendereſt flowers, and devoured the choiceſt fruits. He now wants to return this garden, ſtripped of all the ornaments, and deſpoiled of all the delicacy it enjoyed, when he firſt took poſſeſſion of it.'

The Cadi ordered Feirouz, to anſwer in his defence, and give the beſt reaſons he could offer, for ſo unjuſt a proceeding.

'It is with the utmoſt grief and
'reluctance, my lord, ſaid he, that I
'quit the poſſeſſion of what was
'once dearer to me than life. But
'an accident has happened, which
'renders the enjoyment neither
'pleaſing, nor ſafe. One day, walk-
'ing in an alley of that garden, I
'perceived the print of a Lion's
'foot. Terror immediately ſeized me,
'and I choſe rather to abandon the

---

them, and they allot him a place in Paradiſe, with the aſs that carried Chriſt to Jeruſalem, and the horſe on which Mahomet rode.

* There are no lawyers in the Eaſt, but every perſon, plaintiff, or defendant, pleads his own cauſe. All proceedings are ſummary, and though their decrees are often unjuſt, yet, as the affair is ſoon determined, the ſuitors are ſpared the double mortification of trouble and expence, too frequently complained of in more enlightened countries.

'whole garden to that fierce animal, 'than expoſe myſelf to his vengeance.'

The ſultan, who was preſent, immediately replied, 'Enter into thy 'garden, O Fenouz, thou haſt nothing to fear. It is true, the Lion 'ſet his foot in thy garden, but has 'neither eaten thy fruit, or plucked 'thy roſes. He found it ſo well 'guarded, that, aſhamed of his attempt, he retired, full of confuſion, and will never more diſturb 'thy quiet.'

Theſe words, which were a myſtery to the reſt of the audience, reaſſured the Viſir. He took home his wife, and his fondneſs encreaſed, after ſo ſolid a proof of her virtue, on ſo trying an occaſion.

The Clandeſtine Marriage, a moral Tale.

MR Bridport, a country gentleman, was bleſt (though he was not ſenſible of the bleſſings he enjoyed) with an exemplary wife, and with a ſon who deſerved the kindeſt treatment from him; with that treatment, however, he was never indulged. The old foxhunter, could not, indeed, rationally, find fault with any part of his ſon's conduct, in general, or with his behaviour to him, in particular: but as Charles had no taſte for his father's field-amuſements (he was, in truth, in every reſpect, a very different being) he met with uſage from him which would [illegible] probably, driven him from home, had not his excellent mother happily ſoftened her huſband's ſeverity whenever it was ſhe thought carried too far.

Charles, at an early age, ſhewed a ſtrong antipathy to all thoſe rural ſports in the purſuit of which conſiſted his father's ſupreme felicity, who was as meer a 'ſquire as ever exiſted, and never in a thorough good [illegible] when he was in a [illegible] or a dog kennel. Charles's pleaſures, were all of the literary kind, for which his father, the moſt illiterate man in the country, had not the ſlighteſt reliſh: he had a ſovereign contempt for them: nay, he puſhed his hatred againſt literature to ſuch a ridiculous extreme, that if he ſaw a book in his ſon's hand he never failed to ſnatch it from him with ineffable ſcorn, calling him a d——d pedantical puppy.

As Charles was the heir apparent he was bred to no buſineſs, but he was, by no means, an idle man: to the improvement of his mind he very diligently applied himſelf, and it employed a great deal of his time.

Charles was exceedingly fond of poetry, and had a ſingular predilection for the works of Thomſon. He rarely took a walk without the Seaſons in his pocket.

While he ſauntered one autumnal evening through a corn field, when the weſtern ſky was in a fine glow after ſun-ſet, enjoying the rich deſcription of a harveſt ſcene by his favourite poet, he heard a female ſcream.

Turning inſtantly towards the ſpot from whence, according to the information of his ears, the alarming ſounds proceeded, he ſaw, at no great diſtance, from him, a neatly-dreſſed freſh-coloured girl, ſtruggling with a man, who appeared to be the loweſt lout belonging to a farm-yard. He flew to her aſſiſtance, collared the clown, and fell'd him to the ground: he then, after having told the almoſt fainting fair one how happy he felt himſelf in having been ſo near her when ſhe was in ſo diſtreſſful a ſituation, offered to conduct her home.

The pretty ruſtic was at firſt quite [illegible] to ſpeak, ſo much had ſhe [illegible] by the impudent fellow's rough attack; but as ſoon as ſhe [illegible] herſelf a little, ſhe, with the [illegible] voice imaginable, [illegible] her [illegible] protector for [illegible] aſſiſtance,

ance; adding, that his attendance on her to her mother's humble dwelling would give her an opportunity to redouble her grateful acknowledgments to him. With the man who had behaved in so noble a manner she concluded that she might safely trust herself.

Charles, who had gazed delighted on the personal beauties of her whose screams had drawn him so powerfully to her relief, was compleatly transported with her melodious accents, and could not, without many pauses, and much hesitation, articulate his feelings upon the agitating occasion.

When Charles had brought his fair companion safe within half a quarter of a mile of the little dwelling described by her, he saw her mother advancing, with no small disturbance in her face, to inquire why she had staid so late, looking at the same time rather embarrassed and uneasy, at the sight of a smart young fellow with her. Charles was a handsome, genteel youth, and several of the unmarried girls in the environs exerted all their arts to attract his notice—to be distinguished by him.

Charles, by addressing himself to the old lady (for he had made some unexpected discoveries during his walk in the character of a protector) gave her intire satisfaction, and was intreated by her, on his arrival at her small habitation, to take what refreshments the house afforded. Every sort of refreshment he refused; but he was so highly pleased with his reception, that he begged he might be permitted to return the next day. His request was immediately granted by the old lady, and the young one, with a modest motion of her eyes, assured him, that his company would be very agreeable to her.

Harriot Stainer, when Charles flew to her assistance in the manner above mentioned, certainly appeared to him like a pretty innocent country girl. She always, indeed, had, with her beauty, a very innocent appearance; but she was far from being a female rustic. She was a sensible accomplished girl, and though but just nineteen, had more discretion than ninety-nine out of a hundred among her sex could pretend to. She was also an unexceptionable daughter to a mother who deserved her most affectionate attentions, as she made it the whole study of her life to merit them by her maternal behaviour.

Mrs Stainer, having been obliged by the death of her husband, the greatest part of whose income died with him, to contract her expences, and to move in a very narrow sphere, retired to a small house a few miles from Mr Bridport's castle soon afterwards, and had not been above a month in her new dwelling when her daughter met with so gross an affront, and so generous a deliverer.

By repeated visits to Miss Stainer, Charles grew more and more in love with her, and, at length, prevailed on Mrs Stainer, (who could not resist the pleasure of seeing her daughter married to a man so every way worthy of her, and with flattering prospects) to consent to his being united privately to the mistress of his heart. They were accordingly, soon afterwards, indissolubly united.

Charles, however, as soon as his wedding-day was over, began to think that he had been too precipitate. He became fonder and fonder, indeed, of his Harriot, whenever he stole from the castle to see her; but he became also more and more disquieted every hour while he was at home, lest his father should be acquainted with his clandestine proceedings.

Mr Bridport, for want of penetration, attributed his son's melancholy to his bookishness. Mrs Bridport, whose sagacity was infinitely superior to her husband's, imputed his uncommon and daily-increasing dejection to some secret disquietudes.

 She,

She, therefore, conjured him one day in the strongest terms, to open his heart to her without reserve. "I am your sincere friend Charles, as well as your mother, the uneasiness under which you, I am certain, labour, shall be removed, if it is in my power to remove it."

Charles thanked her in the most dutiful expressions. When he had unbosomed himself, he added, "You see, madam, how much reason I have to be disquieted."

"Do not be too much cast down, my dear," replied the affectionate mother, "perhaps we may find a way, should there be——"

Before she could utter another word Mr Bridport entered the room, smacking his whip, and crying, "Fetch your hat, Charles, and be quick. I am going to drive you to friend Jowler's. You must court Nancy as fast as you can. We have settled matters about you both. You are to be tacked together as soon as the writings are *drawed*."

Charles stood like a statue, riveted to the floor, he could neither stir nor speak.

"Yo, ho, Charles! What ails you? Ar't deaf? Do'n't hear me, boy? You are to be married to Nancy Jowler as soon as the writings are *drawed*."

Charles finding it impossible to conceal his marriage with Miss Stainer any longer, made a full confession, at the close of which his father thundered disinheritance in his ears, and swore in a tremendous manner that he never would forgive him for his disobedience.

At that instant Mrs Bridport fell on her knees, and pleaded in her son's behalf in terms which would have proved successful, if she had addressed them to a man of reason and sensibility, but as her husband had neither [illegible] head to be convinced [illegible] heart to be [illegible] elocution, her words [illegible] upon

the one or the other. The disobedient son was ordered by his father in very mortifying language to repair to the wife whom he thought proper to choose for himself, and his return to the castle was prohibited with the severest injunctions.

Charles bowed, obeyed, and retired, determined never to see his cruel father again. He went immediately to Mrs. Stainer's and made two of the best women in the world as unhappy as himself by the intelligence which he communicated to them. Poor Harriot wept till her eyes were almost swollen out of her head. Deeply affected by her tears, and every way distressing behaviour, and doubly tortured by his own reproaching reflections, he was before the next morning in a very high fever, the progress of which was so rapid that all the efforts of medicine were ineffectual to stop its career. In a few hours he was deprived of his senses, and at the end of the fourth day from its commencement it put a period to his life. The death of Charles proved fatal to his Harriot, and they were both buried in one grave.

Ye Bridports of the age! fathers and sons, who happen to peruse this tale, be not too proud to attend to [illegible] instruction which it contains.

The Unfortunate Lover, or Pleasures of Imagination.

L[illegible] pat I feel [illegible]
[illegible] with same [illegible] desire,
[illegible] methinks 'tis happier [illegible]
[illegible] to know,
[illegible] unbounded [illegible]
And [illegible] ideas to my love.

WALSH.

I HAVE been one of those persons [illegible] have the misfortune to fall in love with every young lady they see, who, by being possessed of any agreeable qualification, has it in her power to inspire that passion, by which means

my

my life has been, till very lately, one continued love ſcene However agreeable this ſtate may appear to ſome, it is, if we properly weigh *diſadvantages* with the *advantages*, not very deſireable, as, like moſt others, its inconvenience is much greater than its conveniencies.

Upon a fair reviſal of my paſt life, I find that I have, by means of my amorous diſpoſition, enjoyed no ſmall pleaſure, nor, on the other hand, has my pain been leſs exquiſite, which I doubt not has been the caſe with moſt others in the ſame ſituation

The firſt perſon who attracted my notice, was a young lady of great merit, a daughter of a neighbouring gentleman in the country, where our family reſided If a lover may be credited in the deſcription of his miſtreſs, ſhe had the beauty of *Venus*, the eaſy gracefulneſs of *Hebe*, the chaſte reſerve of *Diana*, with the knowledge of *Minerva* Fortune however, who is ſeldom favourable to lovers, deprived me of the happineſs which I had long anticipated in the poſſeſſion of this amiable fair one, by a quarrel that happened to fall out ſoon after between our parents, my grief on this occaſion was, my readers may ſuppoſe, very great, and I believe would have laſted to this day, had it not been ſoftened by the arrival of a young lady, an acquaintance of my ſiſter's, who came to ſpend a month with her in the country Being obliged, out of complaiſance as I was the only young gentleman in the houſe to attend them in all their country parties, and, as I before obſerved, naturally of an amorous diſpoſition, I could not fail, by degrees, attracting an [illegible] regard for my ſiſter's companion at laſt, after having, as I thought, inſpired her with a paſſion for me, not very much inferior to that which I retained for her, I found that ſhe had been privately married to a young officer in the army The effect this news had upon me by degrees [illegible]

health, and I was accordingly by my father ſent to Bath for the benefit of the waters In Bath I made an acquaintance with a young lady, that, like me, came for the benefit of her health, or rather of the company, ſhe baniſhed the thought of my late miſtreſs, with as much eaſe as that had done of the firſt in ſhort, I ſucceeded ſo well, that I at laſt prevailed upon her to permit me to apply to her parents, for their conſent to make me happy Every thing was now in a fair way of being ſettled, when my father's being taken ſuddenly ill, called me into the country, my abſence was the means of my being deprived of the young lady, for a gentleman, while I was in the country, had not only diſpoſſeſſed me of the place I held in my miſtreſs's affection, but actually put it out of my power ever to retrieve it, by the indiſſoluble bands of wedlock

I now bid adieu to love, Cupid however ſmiled at my reſolution, having reſolved to torment me yet more. Not to tire my reader with circumſtances, I ſhall only obſerve, that another young lady, not long after, engaged my affections and that I was unluckily diſappointed of the wiſhed-for happy ſtate, by her having the ſmall pox

The many ſcenes I had paſſed with my miſtreſſes, uſed frequently to be the ſubject of my thoughts, nor did they afford much leſs pleaſure in the reflection, than I had received from the reality, as it was in my power to enjoy the reflection of thoſe ſcenes *only* which were moſt agreeable

The pleaſure I enjoyed in the reflection of my paſt amours, naturally led me on to frame new ones in imagination, and by degrees to frame a new miſtreſs, to be the object of my future devoirs, which has been the means of my making a diſcovery, that I think myſelf in conſcience bound to communicate to my readers, as I doubt not I ſhall put it in their power, by means of it, to enjoy a miſtreſs who

will

will [illegible] with all the pleasures of love, [illegible]

After [illegible] which [illegible] to study [illegible] passion, [illegible] all the pleasure of love, [illegible] with the [illegible] introduces you to a mistress, [illegible] always prove [illegible], whom you can never lose by the quarrels or avarice of parents, by a rival, by a husband, or by the loss of beauty, a mistress, who will be always present when her company is desired, a mistress, whose beauty will never fade, a mistress, whose notions will change with yours, whose form will change with your ideas of beauty, a mistress, who can be either gay or sprightly, sentimental or otherwise, just as your humour suits, a mistress, possessed of every perfection that you can form an idea of. Not to keep you any longer in suspense, the mistress to whom I would introduce you, is —— an imaginary one —— Nay, start not at the thought: all pleasure is imaginary. How then can that of love be otherwise? Frame to yourself the fair with whom you would choose to pass the remainder of your life, let her be the object of your constant thought, and you will find, that the pleasure you receive from the company of your *imaginary* mistress, to be much superior to that which would result from a *real* one. When [illegible] you may enjoy the pleasing [illegible] tion that results from the thoughts of being equally beloved by the dear object of your affections [illegible], with her you may enjoy the highest pleasure *imagination* can form an idea of.

Consolation for the Afflicted.

A Poor Dervise, whose feet were naked for want of shoes, made a pilgrimage to Mecca, cursing his unhappy fate, and accusing heaven of cruelty. When he arrived at the gate of the grand mosque of Cousa, he perceived a poor man who had by some accident lost both his feet. The sight of a man more unfortunate than himself afforded him consolation, and convinced him that the distress was greater to be without *feet* than without *shoes*.

The following ingenious Lines have lately been [illegible] *on the Disgrace of the Duc de* CHOISEUL.

DANS ses Traités & dans sa Vie
Réunissant la Droiture & l'Honneur
[illegible] [illegible] son Génie,
[illegible] Intérieur, [illegible] Cœur.
Comme tout autre, dans sa Place,
Il eut grand Nombre d'Ennemis
Comme nul autre, en sa Disgrace
Il vit qu'il avoit des Amis.

PROLOGUE *to the new Comedy of the West Indian. Spoken by* Mr. REDDISH.

CRITICS, hark forward! noble game and new;
A fine West Indian started full in view:
Hot as the soil, the clime, which gave him birth,
You'll run him on a burning scent to earth;
[illegible] devour him in his hiding place,
[illegible] for another chace,
[illegible] country [illegible] claim,
[illegible] commerce, and supports [illegible]
[illegible] humble [illegible] we hope you'll [illegible]
Some [illegible] of a noble mind
[illegible]
[illegible]
[illegible]
[illegible]
[illegible]
[illegible]
[illegible]
[illegible]
[illegible]
[illegible]
[illegible]
[illegible]
[illegible]
[illegible]
[illegible] they can
[illegible] the [illegible]
[illegible]
[illegible]
[illegible]
[illegible]

Rouse, Britons, rouse, for honour of your [illegible],
You would not have us [illegible] and be seen to smile
[illegible] we write not like our fathers — true,
[illegible] our fathers hard to write as you,
[illegible] error of the poet's pen
[illegible] men
[illegible] the times abou[illegible]
[illegible]
[illegible] experiment come out,
[illegible] the [illegible] on the [illegible]
[illegible] Parn[illegible] lofty summit [illegible]
[illegible] mortal camp [illegible] there [illegible] bands!
[illegible] give fair quarter to us puny elves
The giants then will sally forth themselves
With wit's sharp weapon vindicate the [illegible],
And drive ev'n Arthur's magic from the Stage.

EPILOGUE, *to the new Comedy* [illegible] *Written by* [illegible] *Spoken by Mrs.* [illegible]PINGTO[illegible]

N. B. The [illegible] spoken [illegible]

CONFESS, good folks, [illegible] R[illegible]
p[illegible],
S[illegible] for SEVENTEEN HUNDRED [illegible] ONE?
W[illegible] jewels!—there's a precious [illegible]!
To extricate [illegible] brave old man,
And all in love [illegible]
A girl of fortune, [illegible]
B[illegible]
S[illegible] to the refinement [illegible]
That we [illegible] with our [illegible]
I [illegible] and I'll shew
And [illegible] politeness [illegible]
[illegible] Lady Plough[illegible]
Now, with [illegible] rank and title to be free,
I [illegible] catechism—and you shall see,
Wh[illegible] *Dame de* [illegible]
[illegible] that or this,
[illegible] answers Miss.
(She speaks [illegible])
C[illegible], tell me, Cl[illegible], what were our [illegible] and dress,
In th[illegible] strange times of that old fright
Queen Bess? —
[illegible] —
(S[illegible] speaks for Miss)
When Be[illegible] England's queen,
[illegible]
[illegible] Greek t[illegible]
[illegible]
[illegible] heath[illegible]
[illegible]
Pert[illegible]
N[illegible]

[illegible] Greek [illegible] —Our outside head take [illegible]
H[illegible] the inside grave?
No heads [illegible], the are [illegible] quer,
There may be learning in a papillote
Cards [illegible] I, Lady B,
In learning w[illegible] not yield to any she,
Of the [illegible] female university
But now for Lady Blab—
(Speaks as my Lady)
[illegible] me, Miss Nancy,
"What sports and what employments did they fancy?"
(Speaks as Miss)
The vulgar creatures seldom left their houses,
But [illegible] work'd, and lov'd their [illegible]
The [illegible] at Christmas only knew,
They play'd [illegible], and their games were [illegible],
[illegible] and thirty, Put, All fours, and Lanterloo,
They [illegible] of mortals stout and boney,
[illegible] the name of Macaroni —
(Speaks as my Lady)
"O [illegible] my pretty dear—
"No [illegible] a modern [illegible] fair appear,
"[illegible] more [illegible] old dowdy maids and wives,
"Tell how uncer[illegible] beings pass their lives —
(Speaks as Miss)
[illegible] noon they sleep, from noon till night they [illegible],
From [illegible] morn [illegible] game at more or less,
[illegible] encore!—
(Sh[illegible])
[illegible]
[illegible]
We [illegible] from [illegible] to our prime,
To the last moment [illegible]-time
And all [illegible] drum,
H[illegible] empty pockets h[illegible]
Th[illegible] our lives [illegible] away,
Not w[illegible] the nonsense of our author's play,
Th[illegible] true life— [illegible] praise,
Don't snarl and sigh for good Queen Bess's days
For all you look so sour, and bend the brow,
You all rejoice with me, you're living now.

PROLOGUE, *to the new Tragedy of* ALMIDA, *by* WILLIAM WHITEHEAD, *Esq.* *Spoken by Mr.* REDDISH.

CRITICS, be dumb!—to-night a lady sues,
[illegible] Italia's shores, an English [illegible],

Th[illegible]

Tho' fate there b[illegible] her in a pleas[illegible] chain,
S[illegible] to our stage the [illegible] of her train
[illegible] to her birth the [illegible] Britith [illegible],
A[illegible] to her country [illegible] plaud;
From instances [illegible] read [illegible] trace [illegible],
S[illegible] the path her father trod before
[illegible] care [illegible] her cause
And [illegible] applause
[illegible] claim,
[illegible] fame
[illegible]
[illegible]
[illegible]
[illegible] page
[illegible] mind,
A[illegible] chivalry alone taught [illegible] to man
[illegible],
[illegible] the youth [illegible] at-
[illegible]
[illegible] lover [illegible],
[illegible]
[illegible]
[illegible]
[illegible]
[illegible] fair
[illegible] his wishes [illegible]
[illegible]
Honour alone could ga[illegible] her [illegible],
Honour [illegible]
And shall not British [illegible] beauty [illegible]
Adopt to-night the ma[illegible] which she draws?
M[illegible] we contests are [illegible] prize,
Giants and monsters [illegible] rarely rise!
With [illegible] triumph[illegible]
grace,
Attack, [illegible] exterminate the race,
But when a lady tempts the critic war
Be all knight errant, and protect the fair

EPILOGUE *to the new Tragedy of* Almida, *by Mr* GARRICK. *Spoken by Mrs* BARRY.

A Female bard [illegible] her native land
A female should protect—lo! here I
stand,
To claim of chivalry the ancient rites,
And throw my gauntlet at all critic knights,
Nor only for our author [illegible] I come
I rise a champion for the sex at home!
Will [illegible] you, ladies [illegible] the flaunting
crew
And [illegible] Greeks, Romans [illegible] yield
[illegible]
[illegible]
[illegible]
[illegible]
[illegible] their back,
Out [illegible] the dime[illegible], but carry [illegible]
[illegible] back,
[illegible]
pack!
[illegible]
[illegible]

For don't they bargain, when they quit their
homes,
At pleasure's call, to carry too their spouses?
The care of children was no Spartan passion,
And may not we in time import this fashion?
[illegible], nimble finger'd [illegible] rewarding,
[illegible] in the art of dicing, and of carding,
And are these arts beyond our reach or
thought?
Let parents learn, children will soon be
taught
Where, [illegible] with you, ye fair ones, shall we
see,
That R[illegible] virtue—hospitality!
The foreign artist can your smile secure,
[illegible] fidler, or [illegible]
From our dull [illegible]
[illegible] puppet-show,
[illegible] foreign thing [illegible]
[illegible] more [illegible] flesh
blood than players
[illegible] modestly [illegible]
So now, [illegible] and wine, [illegible] act like
[illegible],
M[illegible] and feet, may [illegible] our tongue
[illegible],
[illegible] monsieur! comment [illegible] vous portez
vous?

Once more I challenge all the critic knights
From [illegible] to the wits at White's,
[illegible] volunteers, or hacks,
[illegible] mortals at Almack's!
Should any nibbling critic dare to deem,
[illegible] a chicken [illegible] at
them
A[illegible] to show their teeth, they [illegible] grin
[illegible] come on—I draw my corking pin!
Put in [illegible] our soldiers, sailors, [illegible] our tears,
They only can be conquer'd by your tears
Your frowns may fetter, but your tears can
melt 'em,
The bravest boldest, mightiest men [illegible]
[illegible] 'em
Ay, you may sneer, ye wits, your hearts are
steel
I speak of mortals who can fight and feel!
In peace or war, ye fair, trust only those,
Who love the sex, and always beat their foes
Will none accept my challenge—what
disgrace,
To all the nibbling, fea[illegible], [illegible] race,
Who dare not meet a woman face to face!
The auth[illegible] and our sex have [illegible] their
cause!
Complete their triumph, give 'em your ap-
plause.

The SNOW BALL, ANACREONTIC.

A S lately [illegible] my Cul[illegible]
On Almack[illegible] the Cor[illegible]
A[illegible] her hand she took
[illegible] smiling [illegible]

Thus

Fourth Article

That what we shall not be able to carry with us, you will give us receipts for expressing every article left here, that we may be able to give an account thereof when required.

Fourth Article

There will be receipts given for all the stores, &c. that his Britannic majesty's sloop cannot carry.

Fifth Article

That at the time we are going to embark on board his majesty's sloop Favorite (after concluding the inventories, and delivering every thing to you in proper form) we may have liberty to march off under arms, with drums beating, colours flying, &c. without being incommoded or injured.

Fifth Article

That at the time of their embarking on board the Favorite, they must acquaint the Spanish commodore thereof to agree upon the hour, as the English are not allowed to take arms without giving notice to the said commander, that he may give orders to be observed what they have desired, in order that they may not be incommoded or injured at their departure; but should they do contrary to the above, it will be taken for an attempt, and they will be answerable for the result.

Sixth Article

That to prevent disorder an officer with a few men may take possession of the block-house.

Sixth Article

For to prevent disorder, and to take possession of the block house with regularity and good order, the colonel Don Antonio Gutiarroz will march with all his troops, and will leave in the settlement for the present only a company of grenadiers.

Seventh Article

That the cordage and other material that served for parapets, &c. at the batteries may be put into the store houses, under lock and key, until proper inventories can be taken, or that we may carry them on board the Favorite.

Seventh Article

The cordage and all the materials that served for parapets at the batteries will be put in store-houses, which keys will be delivered to the English till the inventories are drawn in proper form, and they embarked on board the Favorite: granted.

HISTORICAL CHRONICLE.

FOREIGN AFFAIRS.

CONSTANTINOPLE, Jan. 3.

LAST month two Divans were held, in which the Grand Signor manifested his intention of leading his army next campaign. The first was composed of the heads of the law, who represented to the Sultan the danger the capital would be in by his absence; and the second, composed of the principal officers of the army, approved his design greatly; and after they had finished their discourse, his highness made them this proposition: "Can you assure me, and be bound for the same, that at my arrival at Adrianople, or the army, I shall be in security?" Since that time it is said that the Grand Signor will follow the lawyers advice; and, we are assured that his highness has declared, that he will not absent himself from his seraglio, tho' the enemy were at the gates of the city. This resolution has [illegible] a general discontent among the people, who shew it publicly, by insulting the Sultan in the open streets.

The account of the arrival of the third Russian squadron in the Archipelago have renewed our alarms in regard to the Dardanelles. If that squadron succeeds in forcing the Dardanelles, the Grand Signor will then be obliged to listen to the propositions of peace made him by different foreign ministers.

PETERSBOURG, Jan. 18. In all likelihood the next campaign will open very soon. Prince Dolgorucki, commander in chief of the second army, has received orders respecting it. The plan of their operations is said to be known; they intend this year striking a grand stroke against the Ottoman empire; most part of our army is to pass the Danube, and march to Adrianople, and from thence to Constantinople, where one of our fleets is to come by the Black Sea, while our united squadrons in the Archipelago will attempt forcing the Dardanelles, which will not be impossible.

as several foreign vessels freighted for Constantinople, and mistaken for Russians by the Turkish commanders, succeeded in passing those castles, notwithstanding the fire of the Ottoman artillery.

PARIS, Jan 14 We are assured, that since the Duke de Choiseul has been at Chanteloup, a letter has arrived in characters which nobody was able to decipher in consequence of which the Abbe de la Ville went to Chanteloup to ask the explication from the disgraced minister which he gave, that the dispatch came from the Ottoman Porte, in which the Grand Signor communicates to the Duke de Choiseul a new treaty of peace between Turkey and Russia, in which England acted as mediatrix, asking his particular counsel in that respect, as he was not to act without his advice and the approbation of France, to which he added a most flattering eulogium The Duke de Choiseul gave back the character to the Abbe de la Ville, that the king might be able to verify the justness of the explication, and be convinced that the praise heaped by his Sublime Highness on that minister were not servilely solicited

COPENHAGEN Feb 2 Tuesday last being the king of Denmark birth day, it was celebrated here with the greatest festivity On this occasion a new order was instituted by her Danish majesty, called the order of Matilda, to consist of twenty-four persons, the ensign of which is a cypher of her majesty's name, enriched with diamonds.

DOMESTIC INTELLIGENCE

LONDON, Feb 1 Last Monday morning, between nine and ten o'clock lord P[illegible] and lord Milton met behind Montague house to decide a quarrel which happened between them in the Court of Requests on Friday last Lord John C——sh was Lord M's second, and Capt K——ly was Lord P's. When they had taken their ground, Lord P attempted to fire first, but his pistol did not go off Lord M fired next, but missed his antagonist Lord P then fired, and the ball entered Lord M's side, which put an end to the affair. Lord M [illegible] the ball was not [illegible] extracted, but his lordship [illegible]

The real cause of the quarrel between the above two noblemen [illegible] disputed property concerning the bounds of manors lord P[illegible] given his word and honour to lord M that he was not concerned in carrying on the cause [illegible] trial when, in the course of the hearing, the [illegible] from the counsel (upon the judge [illegible]) that they had no authority to [illegible] without [illegible] [illegible]

Extract of a Letter from Paris Jan 21

"The king threatened the magistrates of the parliament, to deprive them of their employments, if they would not obey his letter of jussion, and likewise signified to them that it is in vain for them to make opposition, in hopes that his majesty would withdraw his edict, or at least suspend the execution of it, which nobody was ever authorised to give them any assurance of

"Since this the parliament resolved, that they could not obey the king's letter of jussion, but that they would wait for his majesty's orders with equal resolution and submission

"On Saturday last in the night, the musketeers went to the members of the parliament at their [illegible] houses, and presented to each a letter de cachet, which enjoined them to declare immediately whether they would resume their usual duty, or persist in their refusal, in terms whereof they were to sign Yes or No. They were told at the same time, that their refusal would be considered as an act of [illegible]

"We cannot exactly [illegible] other farther than that some signed Yes, and some No, and many refused to explain themselves declaring, that as private men, they were all submission to the king's orders, but that as magistrates they could not [illegible] are separate [illegible]

"In the morning they went to the first president, and desired to assemble. In consequence of which all the chambers met that day (Sunday) at 4 o'clock in the afternoon, the result of which meeting is not yet known"

"The dispute between the king and parliament of Paris is [illegible] terminated in the banishment of every one of them and the king [illegible] not only [illegible] them to different places, but sent the major part of them to [illegible] to be called inhabited

The Speech of the Speaker of the House of Commons *when he reprimanded* Hugh Roberts, *the Constable and Returning Officer of the [illegible] Borough of New Shoreham in the County of Sussex upon his Knees at the Bar of the said House upon [illegible] the 14th Day of February, 1771*

Hugh Roberts,

"YOU have been convicted, upon the clearest and most [illegible] of [illegible] returning a member [illegible] [illegible] [illegible]

[illegible]

at the very [illegible] of this house, for if the practices of this sort were to obtain the commons of Great Britain, who are now the representatives of the free people of this kingdom, would be merely the delegates of corrupt returning officers.

'In vain have our ancestors been [illegible] carefull to secure the freedom of election by all the means human wisdom and foresight could suggest, in vain have they particularly guarded against the partiality of the returning officer, and obliged him by every [illegible] to a faithful discharge of that trust which the constitution hath reposed in his [illegible], if men are to be found daring enough to send members to this house, who were never chosen by the legal electors.

'You have said that you did not receive the votes [illegible] but only admitted them to poll conditionally, and subject to future revision, as appears by the queries set against their names.

'I think this circumstance alone, was it true, would not much avail you; for I have always been of opinion (although I do not know that the resolutions of the house have gone so far) the practice of receiving votes with queries by the mere authority of the returning officer, and without the consent of the parties, is illegal; I am sure it is dangerous, for if once it be admitted by this house, that the returning officer has a right to receive votes upon terms which are to subject them to his future decision, after the poll is closed, and the numbers known, it will always be in the power of that officer so to manage the queried votes as to return which of the candidates he pleases; and, if he is either an artful man himself, or artfully assisted by others, he will also be able so to do the business, as to make it difficult to [illegible] what he hath done, and more difficult to punish him for doing it.

'But your case does not afford you even this excuse, for it has been proved, that, although you received the queried votes for future discussion and re-consideration, you made your return within [illegible] either, as soon as the poll was over, rejecting, as you declared, all those who had voted for one of the candidates (which amounted to a great majority of the whole) on account, as you alledged, of corruption, notwithstanding you had administered the oath against bribery to all, except one, of those you thought proper to reject.

'There are, however, circumstances in your case which greatly extenuate your offence, and which the house hath, [illegible] pleasure, laid hold of, to mitigate the severity of your punishment; and this they have done [illegible] the recommendation of [illegible] the very respectable gentlemen who composed that committee which, by [illegible] report [illegible] merit [illegible] the thanks of [illegible] the general applause of the public. By a steady attention to justice, and a firm perseverance in obtaining it, they have surmounted a variety of difficulties in carrying into execution a new law, which has formed a new court of judicature for the trial of parliament elections; a law, which, if continued to be executed for the future, with equal abilities [illegible], will [illegible] this [illegible] instance will be a blessing to this country, and an honour to the memory of the person who framed it, and to the parliament which adopted and passed it.

'You have proved, that you were formerly a member of a club, in the Borough, [illegible] which hath [illegible] assumed the name of the Christian Club; a club, instituted for the most infamous purpose, that of selling the borough to the highest bidder; that this club consists of a great majority of the electors; and that the members of it bind themselves to one another, and to secrecy, by oaths, [illegible] writing, and bonds with large penalties; that they carry on this scandalous traffic by a select committee, who never appear or vote at any election, on account of their scruples of conscience, having actually received the stimulated price of the borough, but that the rest of the members of this club vote as they are directed by their committee, and without hesitation take the oath against bribery (as they did in the present instance) and, when the election is over, receive their share of the price which has been paid to their factors.

"You proved likewise that you voluntarily quitted this club in February last, when there was no vacancy, and when you could have no expectation of being the returning officer, in case a vacancy should happen.—It has likewise appeared in evidence, that you acted by the advice of counsel.

"And you have [illegible], that though you may have acted illegally, you [illegible] acted [illegible] wrong, and that you should not have received the queried votes, if you had not been convinced in your conscience that they were all corrupt.

"These are the favourable circumstances under which the house [illegible] considered your case, and, on account of them, have inflicted on you the mildest punishment that the nature of their proceedings will permit.

"And I am, in obedience to their commands to REPRIMAND you for this offence, which I now do. And I am, by their orders, to [illegible] you, which I also do, that you [illegible] paying your fees."

19. Yesterday the lord [illegible] presented their address [illegible] to his majesty at St James's [illegible] the late Convention with Spain [illegible] Falkland's island, a[illegible] and were both [illegible]

Two [illegible]

Twelve hundred thousand pounds is the ... sum expended upon the late preparations for war

The following are the heads of two bills of ... ment preferred to the grand jury against Mr Cornelys ——That she doth keep and maintain a common disorderly house, and did permit and suffer divers ... idle, and disorderly persons, ... well men as women to be and remain, during the whole night ... ing, and otherwise misbehaving themselves ... That she did keep and maintain a public masquerade, without any licence by her first had and obtained for that purpose, and did receive and harbour loose and disorderly persons in masks in the said house and did wilfully permit and suffer the last mentioned persons in masks to make a great noise and tumult, &c

MONTHLY CHRONOLOGER for IRELAND

Sunday, FEB 3

A Fire was discovered in the house of the Countess of Brandon, on Leeson Hill, but before any assistance could be procured the flames raged with such violence, as in a few hours to consume the same. Of her valuable collection of china, plate and rich furniture, scarce any was preserved and it was with the greatest difficulty her jewels and papers were saved

Sat 9 His Royal Highness the Duke of Gloucester, was elected Chancellor of the University of Dublin, which was held by his Grace the late Duke of Bedford

The latter end of last month the house of Mr Smyth T... in the ... co of Cavan was consumed by fire, purposely set to it by some inhuman villain, which they did to ... large rick of hay, and the offices

His Excellency the Lord Lieutenant has been pleased to appoint the following gentlemen to be sheriffs for the ensuing year

Co of Antrim, Hon ... Mc Donnel, commonly called Lord Dunluce

Armagh, Richard Johnston of Gilford, Esq

Cork, Benjamin Bousfield, of Aghadown, Esq,

Clare, Geo Colpoys of Ballycarr, Esq

Carlow, Thomas Whelan, of Mount Wolseley, Esq,

Cavan, Tho Fleming, of Cavan, Esq,

Dublin, John Malpas of Rochestown, Esq,

Down, Rob Ross of Rost Trevor, Esq

Donegall, Geo Nesbit of Woodhill, Esq

Fermanagh, John Haffard, of Garden Hill, Esq

Galway, Thomas Eyre, Esq

Kilkenny, John Wheeler, of ... ath, Esq,

Kildare, Joseph Henry, of Straffan, Esq

Kerry, William Collis, of Ballyn... Esq,

King's Co Gilbert Home of Fermon... Esq

Longford, Edward Nugent of C... lien, Esq,

Limerick Hugh Ingoldsby Massy of Spring Garden, Esq

Leitrim, John O Brien of Dunavany, Esq

Louth, Blayney Townley Balfour, ... of Townley Hall, Esq

Mayo, H... Lynch of Ballycurren Esq

Monaghan, William Smith, of Bally..., Esq

Meath, Tho Trotter, of Duleek, Esq

Queen's Co Richard Sherlock, of Lamberton, Esq

Roscommon, Thomas Wills, of Wills Grove, Esq

Sligo, Sir Booth Gore of Artarmon, Bt

Tipperary, Peter Holmes, of Johnstown, Esq,

Tyrone, Hamilton Gorges, of Ballygaw..., Esq

Waterford, Richard Musgrave, of Ba...een, Esq

Wicklow, Wm Tighe, of Rossana, Esq

Wexford Wm Piggott, of S...y, Esq

Westmeath, Thomas Fetherston, of Carrick, Esq

Extract of a Letter from Kilkenny, Feb 20

" Notwithstanding the ... exam... which the approaching assizes is likely to produce, we are sorry to find that those deluded people called White Boys, are again beginning their nocturnal meetings in this county ... in the face of all legal authority The following is one of their late excursions Between 12 and 1 o'clock last Thursday night, upwards of 200 of these in a ... wretches clad in white uniform, well mounted and armed, attacked the house of the Widow Comerford, near Danesfort in this county, which they broke open and robbed of 80 guineas and two fine handkerchiefs Their pretext for committing this robbery was, to distribute the money among the relations of her deceased husband, who it seems left it to her ... by will, which ... they said he had no right to do It is supposed the above party came from the borders of the county

county of Carlow, as they rode through Gowran, firing several shots.

Jan. 26. His Excellency the Lord Lieutenant went in state to the Parliament house, attended by Lord Visc. Boyne and Lord Delvin. The Sword of State and Cap of Maintainance were carried by the Earls of Westmeath and Drogheda.

In his Excellency's Speech to both Houses, he observed that he met them with the truest satisfaction.—That the affection which his Majesty bears to his faithful subjects of Ireland, and his readiness to concur with them in every measure which may conduce to their prosperity, have determined his Majesty to call them together at this time, that they may take into their serious consideration such laws as shall be found to be immediately necessary for the good of this country.—That the present high price of corn is an object of the utmost importance, and demands their utmost attention, and also recommended to them the continuance or revival of such laws as from experience have proved of public advantage.—His Excellency expressed particular pleasure in being able to inform them, that not only the usual bounties on the exportation of Irish linens have been continued by the British parliament, but that they have been still further extended, a circumstance which he hoped would be productive of beneficial effects to that manufacture.

From the House of Commons, his Excellency did not ask for any further supply, as the duties granted last session of parliament, and which do not expire until Christmas next, may (with very strict oeconomy) be sufficient to answer the expences of his Majesty's government.

His Excellency observed to both Houses of Parliament, that the birth of another prince, since the last session of parliament, is an interesting event, and must afford universal pleasure.—That his Majesty's paternal care of his kingdom requires every return of gratitude, and that he had no doubt from their known fidelity, that they would manifest their sense of his goodness by the temper and unanimity of their proceedings.—That he rejoiced in the opportunity of co-operating with them for the public welfare, and that he flattered himself their endeavours would be mutual to bring this session to a speedy and happy conclusion.

After this speech, most loyal and dutiful Addresses were voted by both Houses of Parliament.

Same day his Grace the Duke of Leinster took the usual oaths and his seat in the house of lords.

Feb. 27. A riotous mob assembled at the Parliament-house, armed with swords, sticks, &c. obstructing the entrance of the members, and endeavouring to administer oaths they tendered, when a strong guard of horse and foot arriving, they immediately dispersed. Two of the rioters were apprehended, one it is said having a book, the other a sword in his hand, and were conducted to Newgate in the evening by the sheriffs and a party of horse and foot.

Directions for entering the Harbour of Balbriggen.

It being found in some late instances that vessels coming into said harbour, in gales of easterly winds have met with inconvenience from not observing the directions formerly given, of keeping a full sail upon them, this further caution is given, that nothing ought to prevent their keeping as press and full a sail as they can carry, as there is an out-draft of water running by the Pier end, which is apt to prove too strong for vessels coming in under slack way, and especially such as have not their main sail set, and their top-sail, if they can be carried, will be of great use, as the other sails are sometimes becalmed by the shelter of the range wall.

It is also strongly recommended to all vessels to keep well in with the Pier end, and to have a cable upon deck ready bent, with a small rope tied to the end of it, and a person prepared to heave it on board a small boat that will be always waiting to receive it within the Pier end, and make it fast to the Pier.

The use of observing the above directions has been fully experienced, for no vessel that has in any sort complied with them ever failed of getting well in, and others, who have slackened sail, have met with difficulties.

Directions necessary to be observed on making the Coast of Ireland, to the West of Cape Clear, being the Observations of a Gentleman, who knowing the Necessity of such, was particularly attentive, not finding any upon such Charts as came in his Way.

For some days before we came near Ireland the sea appeared more or less muddy, but on the second of June the water grew more of the colour of whey, and on the third you could observe, whenever the sea broke, that the sheets of water thus raised, were of a fine deep green colour, which could be best observed when the brake happened in the sunshine. This day the wind was high, and we could not attempt to sound, at noon we were in lat. 50. 42. in the afternoon we steered more northerly, until about 12 o'clock at night, when we concluded the ship was in the latitude of the Cape, then the captain ordered to keep a more southerly course till morning, which was done, and about half an hour past ten they hove to for soundings, which they found at ... 60 fathom. What came

un

up with a rotten brown shelly sand, which glistened a little, mixed with a few of those shells called dentalia, or a slender conick form, about one inch in length, and also a few small pieces and little flints, neither exceeding a line in diameter. The captain concluded he was in the channel, and stood near due north; at ten o'clock we went five knots, and at twelve six knots, when we found ourselves again in the latitude of 51 10 or thereabout. About this time some discovered the land at a great distance, bearing the compass N b L; we made towards it, still keeping somewhat easterly, and we soon discovered it to be Cape Dursey, our course carrying us to a Bantry Bay about six o'clock. The sea continued of the same green colour until about ten, when of a sudden it appeared of a deep blue colour like the ocean, but the more easterly we approached the land, after about two hours easy sail. When we came near enough to distinguish every part of the land, we returned again to our easterly course, to which it was then necessary to add much southing by the compass, to pass the Cape, of which we were a breast about night fall, after having passed the rock.

From this narrative it is evident, there is sounding near five fathoms and to the westward of Cape Clear, which from the colour of the sea, we have reason to think continues a good way further to the west, so that but although we have not been able to try far hence we may conclude that a careful mariner running down the latitude, between 50 42 and 51 12 cannot fail of being well apprized of his approach to the land here.

List of BIRTHS for the Year 1771

FEB 7 HER Grace the Dutchess of Leinster of a daughter.—16 The lady of the Rt Hon Lord Knapton, of a son and heir.—At Kilkenny, the lady of Major Gore of a son.—The Lady of Sir Rob Staples, of a son.

List of MARRIAGES for the Year 1771

FEB 7 STEPHEN Fitzgerald, of Ballyroan, Queen's county, Esq, to miss Hamilton of Ross.—9 Ambrose Lane, Esq Treasurer of the county of Tipperary, to miss Ellen White, of White foot co of Wexford.—14 At Cork, Edward Wilmot, Esq capt of the 40th foot to miss Martha Moore.—The Hon Maj Gen James Gisborne, to miss Boyd, daughter of Charles Boyd, Esq.—At Kilkenny, Edward Baker, of Athenure, Esq, to miss Rose Blunden of Newpark.—19 At Limerick, John Vaunce, Esq to miss Bevan of that city.—25 Jos M'Cree, of Clogher, Esq to miss Martha M'Alpin.—26 Mr James Lyndon, an eminent proctor in the ecclesiastical court, to miss Fitz Stuart of Bow street.—25 Dr Robert Freeman, to miss Jane Burrowes of Cavan.—Mr George Tilson, to miss Sweetman.—Wm M'Vilier, of Monaghan, to miss Hamilton.

List of DEATHS for the Year 1771

FEB 2 AT Tulig, Henry Leader, Esq,—Ardrahan, co of Galway, the Rev James Nicholson, rector and vicar of that parish.—. Ephraim Thwaites, M D.—9 In Aungier street Lewis Roberts, Esq counsellor at law.—12 At Kilreigh, King's co Thomas Pierce, Esq.—14 At Caledon, co Tyrone, Lt Bowie Pringle, of the 40th foot.—16 At Clontarf, Col Wm Wright.—In London, Osborne Jephson, Esq, his fortune which is considerable, devolves to his nephew Laurence Hickey, Esq, who is to assume the name of Jephson.—At Brussels, gen Macartney, a native of this kingdom, and many years in the Hungarian service.—Miss Mary Mitchel sister to Thomas Mitchel of Castlestrange, co of Roscommon, Esq.—Rev Stuart Wilder, whose estate in the co of Meath devolves to his brother the Rev Theaker Wilder, D D and that in the co of Longford to his nephew Matthew Wilder, Esq,—Mrs Gorges, wife of Richard Gorges, of Kilbrew, Esq.—21 At Kinsale, Rev Matthias Spread.—25 John Lyons, Esq deputy clerk of the council board.—26 Mrs Martha Campbell, of Birch horse-lane, aged 105.—Wm Keane, of Clontarf, Esq,—Wm Cooke, Esq.—Mrs Ewing.—28 Mrs White, of Oldmills.—Mr M'Nally, grocer.—Thomas Grant, Esq of Kilworth.—Mr Silcock Glazier.—Mrs Walsh, of Francis-street.—Philip Lyons, Esq,—Miss Cowper.

List of PROMOTIONS for the Year 1771

FEB 5 THE Rev Wm King, A M holds by faculty the united living of Knocktemple and perpetual cure of Kilbolane, in the diocese of Cloyne, with the united rectories and vicarages of Rathkenny, Slathy and Ballynakill, and vicarage of Tedrim, in the diocese of Clonfert, void by the cession of the Rev Dean French.—Benjamin Taylor and Henry Broomer gents elected to the office of town clerk of the city of Dublin, (Henry Gonne, Esq rel.)—Rev Charles Humble, A M collated to the rectory of Derryloran, in the diocese of Armagh, (Rev Mr Cree, dec.)—John Lamy, B L appointed master of the Free-school of Raphoe.—18 William Brady, Esq app capt of the Royal Artillery.—Michael Clarke, Esq capt 42d foot.—Lord Earl Balcarras, capt 10th foot.—20 Wm Hall, Esq app Town Major of Dublin (Thomas Stukeley, Esq rel.)

Lightning Source UK Ltd.
Milton Keynes UK
UKOW06f1935041113

220438UK00016B/1060/P